Picture
Your
Business

PICTURE YOUR BUSINESS

The Way to Extraordinary Performance and Quality

Alan C Clark

To

The memory of my endlessly enthusiastic mother and my unfailingly cheerful father

Published by Word4Word, Evesham, UK

A copy of this publication has been registered with the British Library

ISBN 10 0-9551677-5-2

ISBN 13 978-0-9551677-5-1

Contents

Aims of this Book

Purpose

This book provides knowledge about the Flow & Feedback Diagram, which is an alternative to the conventional organisation chart. It also provides some management knowledge. The purpose of the book and the diagram is to help you start operating your business or organisation more effectively.

Vision

This book will contribute to changing the world of work, making it a more effective, enjoyable and positively developmental experience that enables people to maximise their potential. AND work will be a place where extraordinary customer service is the norm.

Values

The three basic values are equity, quality and lifelong learning.

Equity means justice, impartiality and fairness. Therefore, it is not limited by race, gender, disability, age or any individual differences.

Quality is a basic human value and it is the business word for truth (according to Handy in *The Age of Unreason*). The only one with a vote on this is the consumer.

Learning is about you, even when it is connected with your work. The intention of this book is to recognise and respect individual learning preferences. The writer aims to be a lifelong learner constantly developing knowledge and skills.

Acknowledgements

This book is the result of contributions and support of many friends and colleagues to whom I give my heartfelt thanks. It is after all a system!

Firstly it is essential to acknowledge the contribution to the world of management and quality by Dr W Edwards Deming and his mentor and collaborator Dr Walter A Shewhart. These two people shaped our world. The direct inspiration for this book was Dr Deming's flow diagram that he used in 1950 in Japan and later wrote about in his books *Out of the Crisis* and *The New Economics*, more of which later.

David Montgomery deserves special recognition for igniting the flame of my interest in Deming, which has changed my life. Thanks go also to Henry Neave, formerly Director of Education of the British Deming Association (BDA) for sharing his passion and keeping the flame of Deming's ideas burning. Alongside those for Henry must go my eternal thanks to Val Thomas, formerly CEO of the BDA, whose example, friendship and wisdom helped me through tough times and on to this point.

Also in the late 1990s, I was fortunate enough to meet Colin Nichols and his colleagues at PMI. My grateful thanks to you all for the learning that you shared.

Terry Peterson is not only a friend and colleague but also must be credited with a major contribution to the evolution of Deming's original flow diagram.

To the many former colleagues at University of Birmingham, including Anita Pickerden and Sue Simpson, and Birmingham City Council, many from the latter were students on the Management Development Programme, my grateful thanks. Working with the searching questions of a group of local government managers helped me refine my ideas. Anita introduced me to higher education. She set me a good example of commitment to learning and the needs of students.

Dr Gary Wood inspired the metaphor "Colour Vision not Monochrome".

Recognition is due to Ros Allcott whose outstanding example as change agent in the Criminal Justice System has inspired me. She has sparked many ideas that have led me to write this book.

Learning with colleagues at the Alliance of Deming Consultants and the annual Deming Forum has helped me develop my knowledge over the last 12 years. The commitment to learning and sharing knowledge of one in particular, Barry Mapp, enriched my learning and opened my horizons, leading me to the learning and support available from many friends at the Business Referral Exchange and the Professional Speakers Association.

An important influence on both Barry and myself has been Michael Simmons. His extensive consulting experience in organisation development has influenced many people. His appreciation and humour were very supportive during some tough times. My thanks go to Michael for introducing me to John Kotter's work on change and for his insights in developing the diagram that is the subject of this book.

The Chartered Quality Institute through its Deming Special Interest Group has provided a place to meet to explore how the world of work can be improved. Frank Steer, Michael Debenham and colleagues there have been very supportive. Thank you.

Thanks to John Waizeneker for introducing me to the extract from the history of Royal Naval dockyards, which shows that people have been thinking about the principles of lean management for at least 200 years.

Thanks for the encouragement, feedback and learning from Anne-Marie McTavish, Barbara Chapman, Gary Lennon, Jackie Miller, Susan Cumming and Terry Peterson.

Naturally special thanks are due to Sue Richardson and all at Word4Word who helped me get this book into print.

Debbie Harry and Blondie, Sting and JS Bach provided the musical inspiration for this book.

Finally I want to say a huge thank you to my wife, Pauline, and my daughter, Julie, for their support and for putting up with me while I have been focused on writing.

Alan C Clark
Redditch, Worcestershire
February 2007

Gist

This is the short version of the book!

- A power hierarchy gives a partial picture of an organisation with the wrong focus – the boss!
- The normal organisation chart also omits the customers who consume the outcomes
- People must come first in organisations
- It is the people doing the work who can provide competitive advantage by having ideas
- Quality is a fundamental property of all organisations, not an optional accessory
- Everyone knows what quality means to them and wants to do a good job given the chance
- The manager's job is to create an atmosphere where things *can* happen
- Much management practice is "assuming", or "guessing", or "making it up as you go along"
- A little science helps a lot
- So we get *people-first* scientific management
- System means the bigger picture of a number of things that work together to produce an outcome
- The outcomes or results emerge from all the parts of the system *working together* towards a common aim
- Identifying how value is added for the consumers makes it easier to identify waste
- Waste elimination is a driver of change
- Eliminating waste improves the flow of work, performance and quality
- Feedback is a mechanism that makes systems self-correcting and able to adapt to external changes

- The Study-Act-Plan-Do learning spiral is at the heart of a truly effective organisation and is a feedback mechanism
- The Flow & Feedback Diagram (2F) is a more effective way of picturing a business or organisation than a power hierarchy
- 2F must be used at all levels of an organisation and for all processes like a nested Russian doll so you can "drill" down
- 2F includes the customer or consumer of the outcomes, identifies the value-adding flow and has a feedback path for learning and change
- 2F is a self-adapting way of describing your business or organisation that can deliver extraordinary performance and quality

Colour Vision not Monochrome

Picture this... fun and learning encouraged at work

Picture this... customers *insisting* on your offerings

Picture this... businesses and organisations adapting with agility to changing customer needs and their operating environment

A dream? Perhaps. This book sets out a radically different way of looking at businesses and organisations of every type. It is based on focus on the consumer, customer, client, or service user, on leadership and on explicit learning rather than a power hierarchy. In other words, it sees with colour vision rather than monochrome.

Service and public sector organisations in particular are in a better position to meet the challenge of the "demographic of one". That is, providing individually tailored service to each service user. The new approach can be used for a whole organisation in the public, private or not-for-profit sectors, or a one-person business. Single processes within an organisation can use it as well.

Part 1 looks at attempts in this fast-changing world to change, even just to keep up, which are too often only partially successful or seem doomed to failure. After looking at the root causes, an alternative way to picture a business or organisation in the public or not-for-profit sectors is presented – The Flow & Feedback Diagram. This is both an organisational diagram and change model! It is after all built on the Study-Act-Plan-Do learning spiral.

Perhaps some will view these ideas as heresy and some will be outraged. Tough! After all these years might there be a different and better way?

The ideas behind the diagram are not new and indeed some organisations may have tried them or something similar. Perhaps you have seen this model before but are no longer following it? It may be useful to reflect upon the reasons for that. Hopefully you will find that this book rekindles your interest enough to have another go.

Format: Things to notice

You may have already noticed that each chapter starts with a brief overview and ends with a summary of learning points.

In Parts 2 and 3 you can begin to use 2F both to understand it and as a prelude to understanding your business or organisation better. A chapter is devoted to each part of the diagram. At the end of each of these chapters there is an activity page for you to make your own notes to help hang the ideas onto something that you are familiar with by applying it to your own organisation.

Part 4 contains some suggestions on what to do next, some cautions and a summary.

Part 5 contains the Resources. There is a listing of all the books referred to as well as an index. In the manner of a website, some of the supporting detail has also been included in this part. Hopefully those who want to get to the practical understanding as quickly as possible will find this arrangement helpful. All those of you who would like to know a little more can dip in here as you read.

Inside the back cover is a template for a worksheet based on 2F. You can either scan or photocopy this, providing that you keep the copyright notices, and enlarge it to A4 or A3 to work on it more easily.

Have fun! Do feedback how you get on.

PART 1
PROBLEMS & SOLUTIONS

In Chapter 1 of this first part of the book, we are going to look at problems of rapid change that face people working in early 21st century organisations.

Chapter 2 looks at the root causes of these problems in thinking, typified by the traditional organisation chart. The suggestion is that the causes may lay in leadership, a lack of systems thinking, a hierarchical view of organisations and ineffective feedback channels.

Chapter 3 introduces an alternative to the standard organisation chart. The Flow & Feedback Diagram (2F) is proposed to increase customer focus. In addition, it builds a clear feedback loop into a business or service organisation, thereby institutionalising learning and change. By highlighting where value is added, this diagram helps the endless drive to eliminate waste. This in turn builds an environment more open to change.

Chapter 1 – What's Your Problem?

Chapter Gist

Changing Times

After thousands of years, during which change took generations, change is now getting faster and faster. Too few organisations seem equipped for this.

Change & Sustaining It: People

Organisations do find change difficult and are likely to lay the cause for these difficulties and reluctance to change at the door of people. Is this necessarily the case?

Changing Times

We seem to be told almost daily in the media how fast the world is now changing. The whole environment or context in which businesses and organisations in the public and not-for-profit sectors exist is changing due to political, economic, social, technological and climatic reasons.

It is particularly noticeable that technological change is progressing at an ever-increasing rate. As far as we can tell, for hundreds of thousands of years the tools of hunter-gatherers evolved very slowly. Then, over the 12,000 years since the last Ice Age, farming and its implements evolved and spread. The rate of change has got faster and faster through the Stone Age, Bronze Age, Iron Age, on through the Industrial Revolution to the present day.

Where change has taken thousands of generations, multiple changes now happen within just one generation. Many are familiar with the popular version of Moore's Law stating that the number of transistors in a computer chip doubles every 18 months. The same has been true of the capacity of computer hard drives. However, both these developments will eventually find limits when they reach the atomic level.

Too few organisations seem to be able to cope very well with these high rates of change.

Change & Sustaining It: People

> "If only it weren't for the people, the goddamn people," said Finnerty, "always getting tangled up in the machinery. If it weren't for them, earth would be an engineer's paradise."
>
> Kurt Vonnegut wrote in his 1952 novel *Player Piano*.

Surely everyone has experienced these feelings at one time or another. Problems seem more apparent when change is required.

Continuous change has become a fact of modern life whether in response to changing customer demands, competitor activity or, as above, the operating environment. This is true at a detailed level with attempts to rectify poor quality, performance, products or services, or financial results, and these attempts do not seem to be effective in the long term.

Change just does not stick. Improvements are not sustainable because people keep on working in old ways or at least trying to revert to them. So a new plan or organisation is issued but it never quite seems to work. People getting tangled up in the "machinery" perhaps?

What is it that the French say? *"Plus ça change plus c'est la memê chose"* - the more it changes the more it remains the same.

And what about this well-known quotation:

> We trained hard, but it seemed that every time we were beginning to form up into teams, we would be reorganized. I was to learn later in life that we tend to meet any new situation by re-organizing, and a wonderful method it can be for creating the illusion of progress, while producing confusion, inefficiency, and demoralization.
>
> Attributed to Gaius Petronius Arbiter (~27–66 ad)

Although Petronius was a historical figure in ancient Rome and was probably the writer of the *Satyricon*, there is apparently no evidence of this quotation in literature before the 1939-45 war. It is surmised that it was written by one or more highly educated "wits" who had been drafted into the military and who wished to poke fun at mindless reorganisations. Don't you just wish it were true? And it would be nice to think that the Romans had the same problems as we do. After all has humanity changed that much in 2,000 years?

In addition to failed reorganisations, there are turf wars, empire building and the difficulty of removing barriers to the advancement of particular groups due to gender, race or disability. The trouble is that organisations appear to have hardened arteries that are paralysing change, working against change. Psychology can explain this at least in part, both the way people respond to change and the way people try to impose change on others. It has been said that people do not so much object to change, but *being* changed.

Part of the problem lies in the very human issues of disrespect for other people and ignorance. Much has been written about how people and those who run organisations in particular would be able to achieve more if they treated their staff and managers more humanely.

This short book will not reiterate all of those wise words. However, in the field of *lean management*, which will be referred to in this book, Jeff Liker has as one of its pillars *Respect for People*. Suffice to say that if this basic value is not applied, improvements in performance and quality will not be as great nor will they be sustained.

So... Organisations are not where they would like to be, due to changing situations in which they operate. AND when they come to change, they find it difficult.

This common experience of failed reorganisations is described by that well-worn cliché as being akin to "reorganising the deckchairs on the Titanic". Yes, well, so it is obviously the people alone who are at the heart of the problem. Or are they?

When the whole situation is taken into account a different picture emerges.

Learning Summary

- There are multiple aspects of the world that are changing

- The rate of change facing organisations today, for example in technology, is getting faster and faster

- Organisations need to change to adjust to the changing world around them

- Organisations find it difficult to change and to sustain change

- Might people be only part of the picture?

Chapter 2 – Roots of the Problem

Chapter Gist

Lack of Leadership Processes

Effective leadership processes are essential for change that enables businesses and organisations to adapt in this fast-changing world.

Structures, Systems & Science

Systemic structures influence behaviour more powerfully than we think. Systems thinking is part of a more scientific approach to running organisations, which can work well even in "people-centred" organisations.

The Organisation Chart

Power hierarchies and the functional division of organisations, typified by the standard organisation chart, are part of the lack of willingness to change.

Feedback & a Learning Organisation

More comprehensive feedback is required to enable organisations to change effectively. Often the set of processes that should be in the feedback path to facilitate organisational learning and change are incomplete.

Lack of Leadership Processes

As suggested at the end of the previous chapter, people are only part of the whole situation. However, there is at least one people issue relevant to this book: leadership. Effective leadership is essential for organisations to successfully change and adapt their operations to new circumstances.

Much is written on leadership. Unfortunately, too many of those who should be leading ignore much of this knowledge. People's experience of leadership is too often "top-down"; they are just told what to do by senior management. How often is change based on inadequate perceptions of limited data? Indeed how often is the basis for a particular course of action "assuming", or "guessing", or "making it up as you go along"? Worse still, is change the result of fear, perhaps fear of what might happen to executive bonuses if stock market analysts are not appeased leading to dramatic cost-cutting?

Too often the emphasis in leadership literature is on charisma, traits and style rather the processes by which leadership will be carried out. It seems reasonable that there would be some element of character and behaviour in successful leadership. Insufficient attention has, however, been paid to effective leadership processes. Indeed might leadership be less sensitive to individual variation if there were processes to support it by effectively "hard wiring" it into the organisation system?

Structures, Systems & Science

Systems cause their own crises! So states Peter Senge in *The Fifth Discipline*. He is saying that the systemic structures, of all types, which make up organisations, are a large part of the problem. Outlining the lessons from the Beer Game, Senge states: "Structure influences behaviour ... more often than we realize ... not external forces or individuals' mistakes." He goes on to say that structure in human systems is subtle, a significant example being "operating policies". In this writer's experience, to policy you can add traditions, cultures, institutionalised prejudice and power hierarchies.

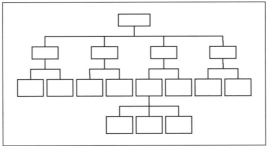

Figure 1

As will be seen below, the conventional hierarchical way in which an organisation chart (Figure 1) describes an organisation is part of the problem. Work is thrown "over the wall" from one functional "silo" to the next with scant regard to meeting the needs of the customer.

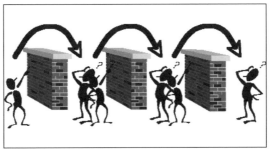

Figure 2

The eminent writers and thinkers Deming and Joseph Juran in their different ways attributed the majority of the problems to the organisation's system. Deming went as far as to attribute 97% of problems to the system! When the trouble is taken to investigate a problem carefully, even scientifically, the root cause may be found in the system and not with an individual or group.

Now the writer is familiar with objections not just to science, but also to even using the word "systems" in connection with organisational issues, particularly in what might be thought as people businesses. "System" just means looking at the bigger picture and from the outside in. Sorry if you don't like the "systems" folks. However, they are there anyway whether you like it or not. If you do not recognise them and act accordingly, your organisation will do disservice equally to your service users and your staff.

The work of Peter Senge, mentioned above, and that of Peter Checkland in his classic 1981 book *Systems Thinking, Systems Practice* both put the case for what are called "soft" or human systems. A system is a whole comprising relationships between its elements that work together towards an aim and whose properties emerge from these elements working together.

Perhaps this all sounds too mechanical or too much like IT or too scientific. But if you are not basing your work with people on systems and science, particularly psychology, you are back to "assuming", or "guessing", or "making it up as you go along". There is room for intuition, but alongside science.

Today we should be familiar with applying even a little science to solving problems. We accept a medical doctor diagnosing our illnesses, often supported by scientific tests. Sherlock Holmes made popular the solution of crime in books, films and TV through logical reasoning and a little science. We have TV dramas based on forensic science being used to solve crime.

The Dolphins Are Back is a case study in applying modern quality management principles, science-based, to cure an ecological disaster. Initially it also illustrated how quick people and the media are to jump to conclusions.

Between June 1987 and March 1988, 740 bottle-nosed dolphins were washed up along the beaches of the State of New Jersey in the USA. There was a predictable outcry that the "usual suspects" were to blame for this and all the visible rubbish and pollution washed up on the beaches.

To cut a long story short, a marine biologist did autopsies on 30 dolphins and discovered that most had died from viruses or toxins released by bacteria in the sea. Further careful study reached the conclusion, based on evidence, that the root cause was predominantly untreated sewage discharged into the sea along the state's 127-mile coastline. The viruses and bacteria fed on this.

The cure was to work methodically, for the next seven years, with the local authorities responsible for the sewage systems. The state's beaches became cleaner than those at any other holiday destinations. This led to a huge increase in holidaymakers, which massively benefited the state's economy. What would managers you know or the politicians have done? Set a target (and avoid dealing with the root causes)?

Returning to issues associated with change and problems in organisations in general, why think that only people cause the problems?

18

The Organisation Chart

When asked to describe the structure of their organisation, many people will rely on the traditional organisation chart or organogram (Figure 1). It is essentially a description of the power hierarchy within the organisation, identifying cascading superior and subordinate relationships. Usually it is based on functional division of the organisation, sometimes identifying line (operations) and staff areas. It has many benefits. On the downside it allows blame to be apportioned to individuals for what are in fact failings of the system. It might appear to be the train driver's fault for passing a signal at red. However, closer study might reveal that the signals had not been designed or positioned to avoid the blinding of a low winter sun. Asking "Why?" might reveal budget constraints on the original installation or a design that had been contracted out to the lowest bidder. Delving deeper might reveal policy decisions at board or national government level based on political expediency.

Peter Scholtes, in *The Leader's Handbook* (1998), calls the organogram the train wreck chart. He tells how, on 5th October 1841, two passenger trains collided head-on in Massachusetts killing two people. The subsequent inquiry recommended a hierarchical organisation structure now familiar in the organogram, which was said to have been inspired by the Prussian Army. Thence it is alleged to have influenced American business practice and by implication the rest of the world.

Hierarchies, however, have been with us for a long time in the church, from monarchs to peasants, and certainly hierarchies were present at least as far back as the Roman and other ancient armies, even if they did not use the diagram.

Whilst the organogram may have proved useful in preventing some train crashes and generally facilitating the development of the industrial revolution, it has its downside. The usual functional division of organisations hinders communication and the flow of work. It also encourages "them and us" thinking. People talk of the functional silos where communication must flow up one functional division and down the next (Figures 1 and 2 again). This hardly encourages timely, effective communications and action.

As a description of an organisation, the organogram is incomplete. There is a serious omission – the customer or consumer of the outcome is not included. Just as serious, it does not show the relationships between value-adding work and non-value-adding work.

According to the report *Lean Profit Potential,* by Peter Hines *et al*. of Lean Enterprise Research Centre at Cardiff University, in many production operations only 5% of activities add value and 35% are necessary non-value-adding activities. Thus 60% must be waste! The perception of this problem is as bad if not worse in service industries or the public sector, because waste is hidden.

Feedback & A Learning Organisation

Organisations are too often run relying only on financial reporting. The "balanced scorecard" tries to remedy this by reporting back across a wider range of key performance indicators. However, this only partially addresses the problems.

Unfortunately, all too often there is no feedback from the front line about how things are going in the market, and those who do bring feedback are not listened to. A number of times the writer has experienced sales people bringing in feedback that was either not listened to or treated with open hostility by senior management.

Conventional management reporting can suffer from the filtering of information as it passes through the multiple layers of management hierarchy. Nobody wants to be the messenger who brings bad news. Or information is too late. Take the case of annual accounts being presented, only to show that the organisation effectively went out of business 18 months ago!

Even when "data", both quantitative and qualitative, is brought into an organisation, nothing is done with it because no processes exist. As Russell Ackoff, writer on systems thinking, explains, data needs to be turned into information, information into knowledge, knowledge into understanding and understanding into wisdom. Here, wisdom means the ability to know if, when and how to act. In the new era of best value in the public sector, the writer of this book has observed local authorities proudly talking about public consultations. When quizzing managers from local government about how they use the data from these consultations, the answer is invariably that little happens. Seldom do feedback processes exist in order to translate market or consumer data into knowledge, let alone wisdom.

By continuing to describe our businesses and organisations using the organogram, we are limiting them. There must be a better way that improves change, leadership and feedback whilst focusing on adding value for the customer, client or service user. Good news. There is!

Learning Summary

- Effective organisational leadership is essential to adapt to this fast-changing world

- Leadership requires the support of effective processes

- Systemic structures influence behaviour more powerfully than is realised

- A scientific approach to running organisations includes systems thinking

- People and systems thinking do go together

- The standard organisation chart typifies the power hierarchies and functional division of organisations that inhibit change

- Feedback processes are required to provide more comprehensive feedback

Chapter 3 - The Flow & Feedback Diagram

Chapter Gist

New View - Flow & Feedback Diagram

The Flow & Feedback Diagram (2F) proposed, is based on the principle of feedback and incidentally on the Study-Act-Plan-Do learning spiral.

Consumer-Focused Picture

The term consumer is used in place of customer to be more general and make it easier to use the new diagram in the public sector and on individual processes. The diagram has a feedback loop that is made up of processes, including leadership, which enable organisations to adapt to change more effectively. 2F must be used at all levels of an organisation, like a nested Russian doll.

Work Flowing - Eliminating Waste

2F highlights the workflow that converts the inputs from suppliers to outcomes received by the consumers. This leads to a focus on eliminating waste to improve the work, thereby adding value for the consumer. Concentrating on waste elimination provides a discipline to maintain focus on what is important. This idea of flow is also central to what has become known as "lean management".

New View - Flow & Feedback Diagram

So we need a way to picture an organisation that includes the customer, client or service user of our outcomes, that clearly identifies leadership process, that includes an evidence-based approach and makes change management part of the way we do business.

This book proposes an alternative approach to describing an organisation, which is based upon the classic feedback diagram familiar in biology and engineering. Figure 3 shows a simple feedback mechanism.

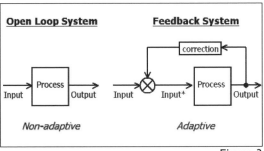

Figure 3

It is also possible to overlay the feedback system with scientific method in the form of the Study-Act-Plan-Do learning spiral (SAPDo), also know as PDSA cycle or the Deming Wheel, running anticlockwise (Figure 4). See more about this in the Quality resource in Part 5.

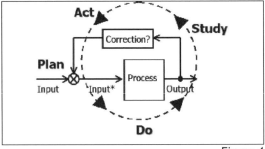

Figure 4

The purpose of looking at an organisation in this new way is to help make it more self-correcting and adaptive. This is achieved by focusing on the value-adding path for the customer, client or service user, and a feedback path that clearly identifies leadership processes and how changes will be put into practice.

As a result, an organisation should improve through an iterative learning process. It is proposed that leadership becomes a strategic process in the feedback loop, which uses a wide range of performance measures that have been through a process to transform performance measurements into information and knowledge.

The Flow & Feedback Diagram (2F), shown inside the front cover, takes this systemic approach. As might be inferred from its title, it shows the flow of business activities from supplier input through to outcomes for the consumer. This flow adds value, thereby creating outcomes for consumers. The diagram includes a feedback path that integrates activities vital for making the organisation aware and responsive to its own performance, the consumer and the external environment. 2F is suggested as a more effective basis for describing and running an organisation.

Consumer-Focus Picture

This book will now generally use the term consumer in place of the more familiar terms customer, client or service user. Deming used consumer in his original 1950 flow diagram (see Part 5, History) thus focusing on the beneficiary or user of the outcomes of a process or sub-process. As a generic term, consumer is more suitable since it does not imply payments are being made. This also increases clarity for internal processes and in the provision of public sector services.

Vitally, by placing the consumer on the chart, it is easier for everyone in the business to comprehend that their purpose is to serve that consumer. This is in contrast to management clichés that abound to the effect that "we place the customer at the heart of our business", when the conventional organogram places the focus on senior management.

Next the diagram focuses attention on outcomes and how those outcomes are achieved for consumers, that is, how value is added. The whole of a value stream, which is the focus of what is called "lean management", of which more later, could be considered to fit into the primary process box. 2F provides a framework within which all the processes of an organisation can relate to each other in order to deliver products or services. The 2F diagram clearly identifies the need to gather and process data from consumers, results, processes, suppliers and the external operating environment into knowledge for effective feedback. It emphasises the need for a strategic leadership role for managers and team leaders who use this knowledge to continually improve and innovate their offerings and processes.

Finally it highlights the place of design (of product, service and process) and implementation or change management in the organisation. 2F must be used at all levels of an organisation and for all processes. The whole organisation is a nested set of 2F diagrams, like a Russian doll.

In the public sector, the author has encountered a statement along the lines of: "Oh, we issued a policy on that ten years ago." However, no change management effort beyond "communication" was put in place nor was the effectiveness of the policy studied. In this way, layer upon layer of policy is built up, much of which could be dispensed with or would not have been necessary in the first place. Building design, planning and change management into organisational processes, and learning from the performance measurements, overcomes this.

It is worthwhile pointing out that in service industries, including the public sector, the primary input is usually information from the consumer (about their needs and wants). The consumer is, therefore, a principal supplier (of information) and also the consumer of the outcomes of the value-adding flow. Thus consumers appear on both sides of the diagram. In practice, the greater overall clarity of the diagram outweighs the slight mental adjustment needed to allow the same people to appear as suppliers and consumers.

Work Flowing - Eliminating Waste

The purple line of symbols across the 2F diagram highlights the workflow that converts the inputs from suppliers to outcomes received by the consumers. After all that is why the business or organisation exists.

Flow is also a central concept in lean management. Lean is a more general name for the Toyota Production System (TPS). The origins of TPS thinking are in Henry Ford's original Highlands Park car plant. Before even the production line, Ford was obsessed with smoothing and speeding the flow of parts to build cars.

In the primary processes, activities should be arranged and continually improved to give the best flow from suppliers to consumers. This is where value is added, and value is in the eye of the consumer! It is what they want to pay for. Quality is part of a consumer's evaluation of value. On quality the consumer is the only one with a vote. A powerful question that everyone should ask themselves about their work at any time is: "Would the consumer pay for what I am doing right now?"

Picture a stream of value-adding activities flowing without hindrance from suppliers to consumers. A study of this value stream in any organisation will find it far from free flowing. Some non-value-adding activities are necessary. The rest is waste, a considerable amount as we saw above. There must be a never-ending search to find and eliminate the unnecessary non-value-adding activities, the waste. *Elimination of waste* is the twin pillar with *respect for people* in true lean management.

Examples of necessary non-value-adding work are checking, inspection or audit. It is often wise to include these activities. The two cardinal rules are protecting the consumer and protecting the organisation from defective supply of products or services. However, any checking, inspection or audit activity in the strictest sense adds no value. These types of activity only add cost and introduce a delay. Whilst the value stream processes do not have the capability to deliver a perfect outcome every time, inspection will be necessary. The drive will be to improve the capabilities of the processes so that ultimately it is safe to remove these activities. The ceaseless drive to eliminate waste serves to overcome complacency.

Okay, you are wondering how the detour into flow and waste helps us with the original problem of poor ability to cope with change. Highlighting the flow of value-adding to consumer puts everything else in perspective. Making waste elimination a priority maintains this focus, and there is a LOT of waste to focus on. This will all be covered in more detail later. Part 2 will help you to understand 2F better by working through each part in the main workflow or operation level.

Learning Summary

- The Flow & Feedback Diagram is an alternative to the organogram

- 2F is built around feedback principles and SAPDo

- The term "consumer" will be the term used

- Using "consumer" focuses attention on whoever is using the outcomes

- "Consumer" is useful in the public sector and when looking at internal processes

- 2F highlights the flow adding value to the consumer

- 2F must be used at all levels of an organisation and for all processes

- Waste elimination keeps the focus on what is important and provides a drive that overcomes complacency

- Flow and waste elimination are part of what has become known as "lean management"

PART 2
THE OPERATIONAL LEVEL

Picture Your Business: Using 2F: 1

The seven main process areas in the 2F diagram are primary, support, performance measurement, understanding consumers and context, strategic leadership, system design and redesign and finally change management.

This part of the book works through the operational level of 2F that includes the primary and support processes. Each of Chapters 4 to 14 is devoted to a part of the lower half of the diagram. Public sector and not-for-profit organisations might like to skip Chapter 13 on profit.

NOTE: Do not be constrained by the boxes! If in your industry or sector there is a unique process area, which overlaps the seven areas above, then put it in. For example, when logistics, warehousing and transportation are a significant part of the system, the primary processes might be followed by a distribution processes box.

Two primary ways are suggested for using the 2F diagram. Firstly as a process framework, the main processes being written into each of the seven areas. Secondly as an organisation chart by entering the names of process owners and teams. As is noted in the origins of 2F, the diagram can also be used for strategy mapping. It can also provide a framework for describing organisations in manuals for ISO 9000 and Integrated Management Systems.

A worksheet has been developed (see inside the back cover) in which to place the names of processes in each of the seven main areas. If there is too much detail for a box, insert a reference to another document. It would be worth considering whether these further documents might not also be in the form of 2F diagrams.

Be relaxed about changing initial entries in the diagram. Overall, working with the diagram is an iterative process. Completing the diagram is about raising questions and learning.

If possible, get the team together to do this.

Learning Summary

- There are seven process areas in 2F

- Add any process areas that may overlap these

- It is recommended that you start with consumers or outcomes

- You can start anywhere if it works better for you

- Overall, working with the diagram is an iterative process

- This is a learning process and you should expect to come up with a list of new questions about your business or organisation

- It is a great advantage to do this as a team

Activity

Photocopy or scan the 2F worksheet on the inside of the back cover and, if you can, it is a good idea to enlarge it on your photocopier or computer to A4 or even A3. If you go to **www.pictureyourbusiness.co.uk** you will find an A4 template for the worksheet in Microsoft® Word.

Chapter 4 – Consumers – First Among Equals

Chapter Gist

Who Are Your Consumers?

Depending on how you are using 2F, there are two main types of consumer: external and internal. The external consumers are why your organisation exists. Therefore, you need to understand them.

Internal Consumers

The next person, team or department who takes the outcomes from a process is an internal customer. Help them help the external customer.

Secondary Consumers & Stakeholders

Think about who else is affected by the outcomes of your business or organisation. Sometimes they are paying the bill!

Who Are Your Consumers?

Who uses the outcomes that you produce or provide? There are three types of consumer. The two main ones depend on how you are using 2F.

When you are using 2F to represent the whole business or organisation, the consumers will be external. These can be individuals, groups of people, businesses, organisations and communities. They are your main focus. Without them your business or organisation has no reason to exist.

It is very important that everybody in your organisation knows who they are and what they are like. You, as an organisation, must also understand their *wants* (which they will tell you about) and their *needs* (which sometimes even they do not clearly understand let alone tell you about).

Internal Consumers

When 2F is being used for an internal process or individual sub-process, the consumer will be the next person, team or department who uses your outcome. Treat internal consumers as if they were external consumers; their wants and needs will help meet those of the external consumer. Help your internal consumers serve the external ones. Find out how you can help them do a better job.

When did you last talk to your internal consumers? Are you supplying them with what they *want* and *need?*

Secondary Consumers & Stakeholders

Secondary consumers can be very important; sometimes they are paying the bill even though they do not directly use your outcomes!

Examples include the parents of students engaged in higher education, local authorities who make grants to students and the whole community including prospective employers, who will benefit from students receiving an education.

Try to keep other stakeholders in mind and remember that this often includes the community. In these times when sustainability and climate change are at the forefront of people's minds, the community may include the rest of the world!

If you are finding it difficult to understand who your consumers are, move on to Outcomes in the next chapter. You can come back here when you are clear about what it is you deliver to your consumers.

Learning Summary

- There are external and internal consumers

- There are also secondary consumers, who have an interest in outcomes and may pay the bill

- Know your consumers and understand their needs and wants

- Never lose sight of the external consumers

- Who else is affected by what you produce or provide?

Activity

Who uses the outcomes from your primary, value-adding processes? Who are your consumers (okay, or your customers, clients, service users, or the next section, department or team)?

Chapter 5 - Outcomes

Chapter Gist

Why Outcomes?

"Outcome" is a more general term and usable in a wider range of businesses and organisations.

What are Outcomes?

Outcomes are products produced or services provided. There are both desired and undesirable outcomes.

Bookends

The outcomes, along with the inputs, mark the extent of a system or process, like bookends. If there are none... !

Start Here

Outcomes are often the most real thing about your work. Usually you know what it is you provide as a service or product. In a complex situation it may help to start here and go back to Chapter 4, Consumers.

Why Outcomes?

The term outcome is used in this book and in the 2F diagram because it is more general than outputs and deliverables, which you could use just as well. Outcome applies whether you produce a product or provide a service. It seems to apply to a wider a range of organisations in the private, public and not-for-profit sectors. In your business or organisation, you can use whichever word provides the most clarity.

What Are Outcomes?

Examples of outcomes are tasty pies, cars, fashion handbags, aeroplanes, arrival at the destination, a report, a set of financial accounts, required information (or an informed enquirer), rested and refreshed (hotel guests), happiness (wide variety here... ☺), patient returned to good health (medical), life saved, education (of students), acceptable social behaviour (offenders), new ideas (from a creative process) and so on.

There are both desired outcomes and undesirable outcomes. At the moment, we are only concerned with what a system or process is in place to produce or provide. Profit is a desirable outcome for a business but in system-speak is a consequence of producing or providing the desired outcome of the value adding primary processes. We will look at other outcomes, including profit, in Chapters 11 to 14.

These are only the known, intended outcomes. There are of course undesirable and unknown outcomes, such as the effects of pollution and the effects of, say, substance abuse, which need to be considered perhaps under Waste (see Chapter 11).

Bookends

Outcomes and inputs usually outline the extent of a process, like bookends. If there is no outcome or deliverable, the process should not be carried out. Absolute clarity, amongst everybody involved in a whole organisation or a process, about what outcome is to be delivered has a positive effect on performance and quality.

As we have seen, the whole Flow & Feedback Diagram can be applied at every level of an organisation. The outcomes, therefore, should be appropriate for whatever level of the organisation, down to a single process, is being studied. When applied to internal processes, the outcome of one process becomes the input to the following process.

Start Here

The outcomes should be the most concrete or real part of your work, system or process. Usually you know what it is you provide as a service or product. A major issue in organisations can be the sheer complexity. It is easy to lose sight of why you are there. As Stephen Covey says in *The Seven Habits of Highly Effective People*, "begin with the end in mind". If you do start here at the "end", go back next to Chapter 4 before moving on to Purpose in Chapter 6.

As noted above, experience of using 2F and its earlier forms has also shown that starting with outcomes may work better for many people and organisations.

Learning Summary

- The term "outcomes" is used because it is more general

- The products that you produce or the service that you provide are the desired outcomes; there are also other outcomes and undesirable outcomes

- If there is no clear outcome, this may explain poor performance or beg the question whether the process is necessary

- The outcomes that you deliver and the inputs that you receive, someone else's outcomes, act like bookends or brackets to determine the boundary of your process or larger system.

- Start here if this is the most concrete part of your system or process and seems to work best for you

Activity

List your outcomes, the products that you produce or the services that you provide. If you are applying 2F to an internal department or process, your outcomes are whatever you supply to the next department or process.

Chapter 6 - Purpose

Chapter Gist

Statement of What is Done for Consumers

The purpose states what is done by a system or process. Clarity throughout a business on exactly what is delivered will yield improvement and help to meet consumer expectations.

Statement of What is Done for Consumers

The purpose of a process states what is **done** by the process, that is the outcome(s) it achieves. Ideally a purpose statement would indicate possible measures referring to quality, cost and delivery time.

For example:

> *Quickly provide error-free minutes, which accurately record meeting proceedings, to committee members and those who are affected or may have to take action.*

Clarity of purpose is one of the most powerful ideas for improvement, whether or not process mapping is undertaken. If people in a business or organisation do not know exactly what it is they are delivering, the consumer may not receive what they are expecting. Not meeting expectations can ultimately lead to losing consumers.

A clear statement of purpose provides a framework within which to achieve the purpose and to assess success. It also provides a basis for a statement about the future, or vision, which is an essential part of leadership.

Using 2F at a business or organisational level may mean that there are a number of different outcomes and types of consumer. Each of the parallel business or value streams will need its own purpose statement. Each business or organisation would then have an overarching purpose uniting these separate streams.

You will find a box at the top of the 2F worksheet (inside the back cover) in which to write a purpose statement.

Learning Summary

- The purpose states what is done by a system or process

- It may refer to quality, cost and delivery time

- Clarity in a purpose statement aids improvement and reduces consumer problems

- Clear purpose enables the provision of best means and makes it possible to assess success

- Parallel business or value streams would each have a purpose statement, and can be united under a single statement

Activity

What is the purpose of the larger system or single process that you are studying? If you are looking at a larger system, you may have more than one value stream running in parallel providing different outcomes. Each can have its own purpose statement. However, all should also be capable of being united under a single, overarching statement.

Chapter 7 – Primary or Value-Adding Processes

Chapter Gist

Primary Processes

Primary processes transform inputs into outcomes, products and services for consumers.

Value-Adding Activity

Activity that transforms inputs into outcomes is something that adds value in the eyes of the consumers and which they would "pay" for.

Importance of Adding Value

By identifying value-adding processes, 2F focuses organisations on and highlights the importance of the activities that are the reason for its existence.

Primary Processes

The primary processes are those activities directly involved in taking inputs and transforming them into products and services. A simple example is making a pie, which may involve selecting, preparing and mixing the ingredients, putting the pie together and baking it.

Value-Adding Activity

In a business such as car manufacturing, making components and car bodies and assembling them along with bought-in or sub-contracted parts to produce a car are all value-adding activities. The consumer will value and pay for this activity.

Whilst they probably realise other activities are necessary, consumers may not be keen to pay for them. Non-value-adding activities would be the accounting, cleaning, payroll, HR, maintenance, provision of IT infra-structure, facilities management, heating, lighting and so on. Clearly many of these are not even remotely involved in turning raw materials and components into cars. The people making the cars, though, are pretty keen customers of the payroll process!

In software development, the primary process might involve understanding requirement, business analysis, planning, design, coding, debugging and final testing. A hot debate might surround whether final testing added value or was just a necessary (if not essential!) non-value-adding activity. This is the point; questions are stimulated about processes or sequences of processes rather than accepting the way it has always been done.

Importance of Adding Value

In some businesses or organisations, the organogram can create a false impression of the relative importance of the different functional divisions. Let us be clear: only the functional division that adds the kind of value which consumers will "pay" for is important *and* essential, whether in production or service provision. The other functions are cost adding. They may well be necessary non-value-adding activities, or even legally mandatory and thus essential, but they are not as important as activities that add value.

When it comes to cost-cutting, it sometimes seems that the head count in production or the call centre is the one where the cost-cutting axe will fall.

This is at best shortsighted. Value-adding activities actually represent a very small proportion of total activities.

The power of 2F is to bring into focus the consumers and the areas that add value. It raises the possibility of using lean management concepts to move from cost-cutting to the elimination of waste.

Part of the overall primary processes or the value stream may have been outsourced or sub-contracted. As such, this activity may be considered sub-processes within this area. If they are adding value, these people might be thought of as "workers in the process" and more like partners. This is despite the fact that the purchasing department calls them suppliers. The workflow and relationships with these providers or sub-contractors will require great care and knowledge in order to produce the best performance and quality over the long term.

Learning Summary

*   Primary processes transform inputs into consumer outcomes

*   Consumers will "pay" for value-adding activities because they produce the outcomes they require

*   2F bring into focus the importance of areas that add value for consumers

*   Encourage partnerships with sub-contractors or outsource providers who are part of primary processes

Activity

What are your primary processes? Include those that are sub-contracted or outsourced if they are part of the value-adding stream.

Chapter 8 – Inputs

Chapter Gist

What are Inputs?

An input is what starts primary processes working. Inputs may be objects or information.

Information

In the service sector and many parts of the public sector, information is the most important input, whether verbal, written or in electronic form.

Bookends

The inputs, along with outcomes, mark the extent of a system or process, like bookends. Outcomes from previous processes are inputs to internal processes.

What are Inputs?

An input is what starts primary processes working. The primary processes may be being prepared in some way, like bringing an oven up to temperature, but no value can be added.

The input might be considered both the starting signal and an indicator to look for timesavings or waste elimination. If the oven is very large and operates at a very high temperature, the opportunity for improvement might be significant, possibly requiring new technology.

Inputs take many forms, physical objects such as raw materials, ingredients or components, or partially completed products and services. In health care, inputs might be an injury, illness or abnormal behaviour.

The issue of behaviour leads us to consider inputs that are not objects, and leads us into service and public sectors where information is often the input.

Information

The information to start the primary process may be in written form, such as a letter, report or case file, or it could be verbal, perhaps a face-to-face or telephone enquiry, or it may be electronic. It could even be visual, for example smoke or flames from a fire.

There are less tangible inputs, such as a need for education. In professional services such as law the input may be abstract, maybe a feeling that a person had been wronged.

Bookends

As stated above, outcomes and inputs usually outline the extent of a process, like bookends. The clarity of the process boundary helps everybody deliver better performance and quality. Inputs to internal processes are the outcomes of previous processes.

The quality of inputs can have significant effects on the efficiency of a process and the quality of the outcomes. Performance measures on inputs may be important to help us understand how inputs affect quality and performance.

Learning Summary

•   Inputs are required for value-adding to start in primary processes

•   Inputs may be physical objects or less concrete things such as behaviours and information

•   Information can be the most important input in the service sector and many parts of the public sector

•   The inputs that you receive, someone else's outcomes, and the outcomes that you deliver determine the boundary of your process or larger system

Activity

What are the inputs to your primary processes?

Chapter 9 – Suppliers

Chapter Gist

Suppliers

Logically the suppliers of the inputs to your primary processes will be the next people upstream from you.

Suppliers in Service and Public Sectors

Suppliers in service and public sectors are often the consumers supplying information.

Partnership

Encouraging partnerships with your suppliers may lead them to help you develop your consumer offerings.

Suppliers

Working round 2F and following on from Chapter 8, the next area to cover is suppliers. Now, if you are making cars, supertankers or tasty pies, it is pretty clear that suppliers are the ones who provide raw materials components or ingredients. Logically the suppliers of the inputs to your primary processes will be the next people upstream from you. Inside an organisation, they will be another process.

In service organisations and much of the public sector, the suppliers will include the consumers, when they are providing information about their wants and needs.

In 2F, sub-contractors and providers of outsourced services are suppliers when they supply the inputs to the primary process, otherwise they are workers in the process.

Partnership

Just as an aim in sales is to build a relationship with the consumer, it pays to build a relationship, or a partnership, with your suppliers. The better they understand your business, the more they will be able to help you develop your products and services.

Learning Summary

- Suppliers provide the inputs to the primary processes

- In service industries and the public sector, often the consumer is the supplier of information to the process

- Encourage partnerships with your suppliers

Activity

Who are the suppliers of the inputs to your primary processes? They will be the next people upstream from you. In service organisations, they will include the consumers when they are providing information about their wants and needs.

Chapter 10 – Support Processes

Chapter Gist

Your Bridge

Support processes are the piers of a bridge holding up your primary processes.

What Are They?

Support processes are necessary non-valuing processes required for primary processes to operate. The consumers of their outcomes will be in the primary processes.

Outsourcing Core Competencies?

Some support processes may be core competencies. When outsourcing, great care is required in selecting partners.

Your Bridge

Support processes are like the piers of a bridge carrying the primary processes. If you take them away the bridge, in this case the provision of products and services, will collapse. This again exposes the risk of taking an across-the-board cost-cutting approach. Cutting back on essential support processes is just as dangerous to long-term performance, quality and survival as cost-cutting in primary processes.

What Are They?

As above in determining what is a primary process, the question is: "Would the consumer want to buy the outcome from this process?" A second question is: "Is this directly supporting Primary Processes?" Often the consumers of the outcomes from support processes can be found in the primary processes.

Necessary non-value-adding processes can, as shown in Chapter 11 on Waste, account for a large proportion, perhaps 50% or more, of overall activity. Depending on the individual business or other organisation, these processes may include bookkeeping, payroll, financial audit and accountancy, HR, quality audit, communications and IT infrastructure, maintenance, facilities management, catering, cleaning, security and many more. Training is an interesting further possibility as part of induction or the development of staff and managers. Training may also occur in Change Management Processes (see Chapter 19), when new or different skills are required to complement systemic changes.

The consumers for each of these processes or groups of processes are primarily those in the primary processes. A 2F diagram could describe each of these support processes.

Outsourcing Core Competencies

Careful thought needs to be given before outsourcing support processes. An important consideration is whether a particular support process is a core competency of the business.

Pure cost or cash flow is not the only consideration for outsourcing support processes. Can outsourcing tap into greater expertise or better technology?

On the other hand, it may not be advisable to outsource support processes if this makes the organisation slower to respond, less flexible or less able to meet consumer needs. This may point to the need to carefully consider which criteria to use when selecting partners.

Equally, outsourcing may limit the pool of staff and managers that the organisation might draw on for the future.

Linked to this is whether the culture and values of the industry to which processes are outsourced are compatible with that of the organisation.

Learning Summary

- Support processes are the piers of the bridge that is your primary process

- They are necessary non-valuing processes required for primary processes to operate

- Often the consumers of the outcomes from support processes can be found in the primary processes

- Support processes may be core competencies; outsource with care and make sure partners are a good match for your organisation

Activity

What are your support processes? Include any that are sub-contracted or outsourced.

Chapter 11 – Waste

Chapter Gist

Waste: A System Outcome

Waste is an outcome of the whole organisational system.

Cost-Cutting: What a Waste!

Research indicates that, across a range of sectors, on average half of costs are non-value-adding and unnecessary.

Constant Gardening

Waste, like garden weeds, keeps appearing, often in new forms, requiring ongoing work to eliminate it.

Waste Elimination: Changing Culture

Introducing waste elimination engages everybody in the organisation in change, helping to make the culture one where change is the norm.

Ways to Start Eliminating Waste

There must be a methodical approach to waste elimination, including awareness of the eight wastes, making "Waste Walks" and 5S. The latter not only helps reduce waste, it also makes problems more easily visible.

Waste: A System Outcome

Waste is activity that neither adds value that consumers would "pay" for nor is necessary non-value-adding, such as paying staff and meeting legal requirements. What is perhaps not so obvious is that waste is a result of how the whole organisational system operates, part of the way all the elements work together. Remember that policies are part of the system and may need changing. Further, to remove waste requires a methodical approach based on knowledge and understanding.

Cost Cutting: What a Waste!

Hines, Silvi and Bartolini show, in *Lean Profit Potential*, that in a production environment only 5% of time was spent in value-adding activity and 35% in necessary non-value-adding activity, leaving 60% waste. In environments such as offices, retail or distribution, the time wasted can be even worse, with only 2% of time being spent in value-adding activity and 49% in necessary non-value-adding activity, leaving 49% waste. Across a range of sectors Hines *et al*. report that on average over 50% of costs are waste. This report can be downloaded from the publications page at **www.leanenterprise.org.uk**

It is evident from the above that it makes no sense to cut costs blindly across the board, since value-adding and necessary support activities may be damaged. Your consumers will not understand that you have saved X%, only that the quality has fallen. Remember they are the only ones with a vote on quality (see Quality in Part 5). At the same time, activities that add no value and are not necessary will only be reduced by a percentage rather than eliminated completely.

Detailed knowledge and understanding is required about each of the processes that make up the whole system. The people who have this knowledge are those working in the processes.

What's in it for them? *It should make life easier and secure their jobs.* In the long term some types of job *will* disappear. The nature of the work *will* change but people *will* still be required. They need to feel that the organisation will look after them, if they will be expected to use their experience, ingenuity and imagination to help make a better organisation. Trust needs to be built up.

Abraham Maslow's hierarchy of human needs builds from a base of satisfying physiological needs, through levels of safety, social and esteem needs to self-actualisation. Self-actualisation here means making the most of their abilities and being the best they can. Using fear threatens needs at a lower level like safety, which he found caused people to think only about those needs. Thus using fear is particularly counterproductive in a creative situation.

People are not stupid; it is only management who think their staff cannot spot an attempt at *manipulation*! This is discussed further in Part 5, Management: Lean or Mean.

Constant Gardening

Waste, like weeds, keeps appearing, often in new forms. Likewise waste elimination is a never-ending task and should become part of the way organisations do business.

The Internet provides an excellent up-to-date example of this. It is awonderful medium: communication, connectivity and access to knowledge now bring all manner of waste, such as spam (junk emails) and threats from computer viruses, "trojans" and "phishing", all of which require counter-measures. New problems or threats seem likely to emerge in the future, so you can never stop. It is now necessary for every computer with Internet access to have a firewall and continually updated antivirus software. Without these there would be even greater waste. These countermeasures do not add value for consumers, even though they are very *necessary*.

Waste Elimination: Changing Culture

Culture is yet another systemic outcome!

Culture develops over time and for this reason many "culture change" initiatives are doomed to failure. As has been seen, change itself is difficult; how much more difficult then to change the culture. Change the system.

A useful place to start is by introducing waste elimination as part of the way an organisation does business. The benefit is that the whole organisa-tion should eventually become used to looking for change opportunities, small and large. Part of this is the introduction of a suggestion scheme, but beware the use of incentives (see extrinsic motivation under The Motivation

Situation in Chapter 14).

Methodical waste elimination, see below, and suggestion schemes would stimulate the creativity of everyone in a way that is difficult to imagine in a top-down culture. Involving staff at all levels in change, making change a way of life, provides a bonus! Removing waste not only lowers cost, it also reduces complexity, which has a huge multiplying effect on the smooth running of the whole system. Perhaps change as it has been known might become unnecessary.

Ways to Start Eliminating Waste

Familiarity means that it can be difficult to spot waste. To help recognise waste, eight types have been suggested:

1. Excess activity (too much, too soon; overproduction)

2. Work in progress and stock

3. Unnecessary processing (things consumers don't want)

4. Excess body movements

5. Mistakes or defects

6. Waiting or delays

7. Unnecessary transport

8. Not using people's minds, not listening to them, their fear of speaking out

Encourage everyone to take a "Waste Walk" through processes and premises to see how much waste can be identified.

It is in the daily routine that a great long-term difference can often be made. The 5S approach has been found to develop good working practices. The five S's are:

Sort – tools, equipment, materials, etc., in the work area, keeping only essential items, storing or disposing of the rest

Straighten or *Set in order* – a place for everything and everything in its place

Shine – going that extra mile to keep the workplace clean

Standardisation – ceaseless development of best practice

Sustain self-discipline – encouraged through ongoing induction training, through promotion and by management and team leaders setting a good example

This is much more than good housekeeping; it is part of *visual management*. Problems or mistakes can be seen more quickly and rectified in an uncluttered workplace, which benefits both the consumer and the organisation.

Learning Summary

- Waste is activity that neither adds value nor is necessary

- Waste is an outcome of the whole system

- On average more than 50% of cost in organisations is waste

- Waste elimination, like weeding the garden, is a never-ending task

- Methodical waste elimination helps to develop a change-oriented culture

- Waste elimination can also lead to things running more smoothly

- Take a "Waste Walk" through your processes

Activity

What processes or methodologies are used in your business or organisation to eliminate waste? What would a "Waste Walk" through your primary processes identify?

Chapter 12 – Cost

Chapter Gist

Cost

Cost is an outcome of the system or process. Treating people as a variable cost, as part of a financial equation, misses the point and an opportunity. People *are* an organisation and its competitive advantage.

New Money

Knowing the total cost of each part of the organisation and running as a cash accounting business is more effective.

Cost

Cost like waste is an outcome of the system or process. You can reduce cost by eliminating waste. This means that you can release resources to be used more productively.

In businesses you can probably have more output, more sales, better quality and more profit. In the public and not-for-profit sectors it should mean delivering better quality services with lower environmental impact, possibly at lower cost.

A problem that comes with a common application of Return On Investment (ROI)-based thinking is that cost reduction means reduction in employment. This follows from allocating your costs and overheads per employee. There is an assumption that people are a variable cost to business, when in reality they are a fixed cost. You may be able to flex with demand using temporary staff or by sub-contracting. Alternatively you can ask your consumers to come back when you have the capacity. If you are good at what you do, they may well return.

Here's the big question. Having spent all those years gaining knowledge, experience and building trusted relationships with staff and managers, why would you pay them to take all this away by making them redundant?

The problem comes from trying to apply financial thinking to human beings. Yes, of course, they cost money to employ. Here's the thing, though: *people are the organisation*, and that is everyone not just management.

Therefore, treating them with respect, as human beings, comes first before looking at any new approach to management. If you cannot, you might as well stop reading this or any other book.

New Money

In late 2006 Toyota was worth almost as much as the next four largest motor manufacturers. According to Waddell and Bodek, in *The Rebirth of American Industry*, the failure to emulate this and apply lean management generally is down to the financial approach. So forget ROI, look at total cost and run as a cash accounting business. An interesting finding.

Learning Summary

- Cost is an outcome of the system or process

- The people are the organisation and its competitive advantage

- Know your total operating cost and run as a cash accounting business

- Read Wadell and Bodek

Activity

What is the total cost of running the process, team, department, division or organisation?

Chapter 13 – Profit

Chapter Gist

Businesses

Profit is vital in a business; it is an outcome of the system every bit as much as the offering or outcomes for the consumer. Balance is required between the uses of profit.

Processes

Processes are required to determine the business needs for profit and the various types of re-investment.

Businesses

Let us be clear, businesses need to make a profit otherwise they are hobbies or charities. Here's the thing: profit is to business like air or blood is to a human being. It is vital. In order to survive in the long term, profit provides a return for all the resource invested. It is also a source of money to: develop new products and services; replace plant, equipment and premises; and develop all the people in the business. We need it. Definitely.

Just as air and blood are vital for human beings, profit is essential for a business to survive. However, you shouldn't think about profit to the exclusion of all else, otherwise you will loose the plot. The consumer should be your focus, for if you do not serve them there will be no business. The better value that consumers perceive in the offering, the happier they will be. Consumers might buy more, they might tell their friends, and they might even be prepared to pay a higher price! Naturally businesses need to be set up in such a way that they can make a profit. Once operating, though, there should be a balance: focus constantly on the consumer while continually improving and innovating the offering and the delivery subsystem. It often seems that profit becomes an obsession to the exlusion of a balanced view that also includes re-investment in the business; this also means in the training and development of all of the people.

Public sector and not-for-profit organisations should also be consumer focused and continually improve and innovate products, services and processes. Society is constantly developing new needs for which resources are required.

Processes

Processes are needed to identify whether enough profit is being produced, depending on the type of business or sector. Is the return sufficient for the resources employed? How are the requirements for investment in new and improved products or services assessed? How are the business's training and development needs assessed?

What is of interest in 2F analysis is what processes exist to study profit and the detailed needs of the business to re-invest it.

Learning Summary

- It is a business rather than a hobby or pastime when it makes a profit

- Profit is an outcome of the whole system

- Excess concentration on profit may distort other outcomes, like those for the consumer, and lead to diminishing returns

- Balance profit with consumer focus and continual improvement and innovation

- Processes are required to ensure that appropriate profit is generated for its many uses

Activity

How does your business review profit and the balance of its application between the various needs of the business?

Chapter 14 – Morale & Motivation

Chapter Gist

Outcomes of the System

Morale and motivation are outcomes of an organisation's systemic structure.

The Motivation Situation

Motivation has been divided into extrinsic, based on rewards and punishment, and intrinsic, driven by people's internal satisfaction. Why should your staff care about your business or organisation?

Outcomes of the System

"Outcomes of the system?" I hear you ask. Think about it. Are morale and motivation low because you just cannot get the staff these days or because you have not had enough motivational "rah-rah" sessions? Might morale be low because of the whole situation in an organisation? The "whole situation" is the system. We are back to the Peter Senge statement that *systemic structure influences behaviour*. Therefore, to improve morale, the system needs to be changed, which is the responsibility of management with the help of the staff.

This requires management to question themselves and give honest answers. What roadblocks are management building to demoralise people? What are the stated values in your workplace and are they being put into practice? One process is for management to consistently set an example by putting the values into action. Another process is known as "management by walking about"; getting out of the office and really getting to know them rather than treating them as cogs in a machine.

The Motivation Situation

Many management books convey the impression that you can motivate staff. Let us just consider that for a moment. Motivation is a dynamic state of people *wanting* to do something. Peter Scholtes in *The Leader's Handbook* says it is the ultimate management conceit that they can motivate anyone; they can demotivate, though. People do things for their reasons not yours. Get over it.

Motivation has been divided into two types: extrinsic, the use of rewards and punishment, and intrinsic, wanting due to some internal desire that brings personal satisfaction.

The problem with extrinsic motivation is that rewards or punishments become the focus not the task. Deci and Ryan suggest that intrinsic motivation requires active encouragement from the whole situation. Abraham Maslow again. In the section on Quality (see Part 5) the writer argues that people know what quality is and, given the chance, want to do a good job.

So why would anyone care about the organisation besides you, the management? Why should your staff care?

Learning Summary

- It is systemic structure that influences behaviour

- Management is responsible for the system including the roadblocks to good morale and motivation they build

- There are two types of motivation: extrinsic and intrinsic

- Extrinsic motivation uses rewards and punishment to get people to do things

- Intrinsic motivation requires active encouragement and leads to people doing things because they want to

Activity

How do you know what morale and motivation are like?
What are your processes? How does the whole situation in
your organisation encourage people to do a good job? Write
this here and summarise them on the 2F worksheet.

PART 3
THE STRATEGIC LEVEL

Picture Your Business: Using 2F: 2

This part of the book works through the strategic level of 2F that includes process areas for performance measurement, understanding consumers and context, strategic leadership, system design and redesign, and finally change management. Chapters 15 to 19 therefore cover the upper half of the diagram, the feedback path.

The word "strategic" may seem a bit over the top for some businesses or organisations. In this book it is used to mean long-term intentions to reach a certain goal. Strategy will be based on a broad set of assumptions and an approach to the way business operates.

Be prepared for some tough questions when completing this part of the diagram. Organisations can find it hard to identify any connected processes at this strategic level, this feedback loop. The absence of these processes may explain why the organisation finds it difficult to respond to consumer needs or to change effectively and sustainably. These processes may of course be informal, perhaps in someone's head, which makes them no less valuable. It helps to recognise that they exist, for this may prompt their improvement.

An individual internal process using 2F may have limited freedom within the larger primary processes serving consumers. The process owner or team leader can still use the framework to drive larger-scale continual improvement and innovation of the process. The aim of an individual process must still be consistent with meeting the wants and needs of the final consumers.

Chapter 15 – Performance Measurement

> ## *Chapter Gist*
>
> ### *Performance Measurements or the Processes?*
>
> This chapter offers information to help you choose how to use the 2F worksheet.
>
> ### *Why Performance Measurement?*
>
> Performance measurement provides knowledge as a basis for decisions, reducing the tendency for people to manage on "gut feel".
>
> ### *The Trouble with Totals & Averages*
>
> Real-world numbers show apparently random variations. Using performance measures in the form of totals and averages hides knowledge they contain about how systems and processes are working.
>
> ### *Process for Dealing with Real-World Numbers*
>
> The process behaviour chart is proposed as a process for getting knowledge from real-world numbers.
>
> ### *Some Possible Performance Measures*
>
> Some examples of possible performance measures are suggested to give a fuller picture, rather than relying on financial figures alone.

Performance Measurements or the Processes?

The 2F worksheet offers the choice of writing in the names of measurement processes or of the performance measures for each part of the system. This chapter will hopefully help you choose which way works best for you.

Five headings for performance measures are proposed: Consumers, Results, Process, Inputs and Suppliers. At the end of this chapter some possibilities will be suggested for each of these.

Why Performance Measurement?

Much management practice appears to be based on "assuming", or "guessing", or "making it up as you go along". Possibly this is because a myth has grown up that knowing the answers and making decisions is what managers are paid for.

When people try to make decisions or improve things, human nature, the PEA syndrome, can get in the way:

Perception – There are long-term filters of our view of the world; nobody sees the world or events the way things really are. Everyone has been conditioned by their life experiences.

Emotions – Feelings, changing from moment to moment, are just part of the human condition and affect the way we think and act.

Assumptions – These are made all the time, including conclusions that we jump to, about the way things happen or the way things work, because life is complicated.

So people in business and organisations have resorted to figures or numbers to help them out and make apparently more informed decisions.

The Trouble with Totals & Averages

There is a tendency to do very limited things to get knowledge and under-standing from figures. Usually totals and averages are compared with plan or results from previous periods. Plans and budgets are fine but are only statements of intent. These figures or numbers represent a complex human-technical system that "speaks to you". Given the amount of wishful thinking in many budgets, why do you think they are going to be met with any sort of accuracy? Is that why accountants have contingencies? Sorry everyone!

The trouble with using totals and averages is that they hide what is happening in real-world numbers. You may have noticed that they seem to randomly vary or fluctuate from point to point. What is required is a way of dealing with the fluctuations while also drawing out messages hidden in these data. The main problem is how to sort out probable signals for action from the likely noise of random variations.

And – you won't like this – how do you know it is *safe* to use any measurements to predict the future behaviour of a system or process?

Process for Dealing with Real-World Numbers

The graphical approach proposed here is well proven and was developed in the 1920s by Dr Walter Shewhart.

- Stop using tables of totals and averages alone

- Put the individual measurement in a graph against time

- Draw on the average and two decision lines limits (see Wheeler's book, referred to below, for how to do this).

Minor Repairs Completed within 28 Days

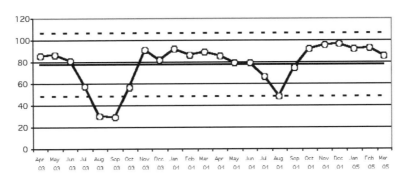

This graph tells much more about how this process is working than simple annual totals or averages in a table. It has turned measurements or data into knowledge and hopefully better understanding. What do you notice in the graph?

This book uses the name given by Dr Donald Wheeler to these graphs: process behaviour charts. Read more about this at **www.spcpress.com** or in Dr Don's book *Understanding Variation: The Key to Managing Chaos.*

Process behaviour charts tell you whether:

1. Your numbers are safe to use, i.e. whether they are stable enough to predict future performance

2. There is a signal for action in your numbers

3. Any changes you make have made a significant difference

Some Possible Performance Measures

As stated in Chapter 2, Roots of the Problem, organisations are too often run relying primarily on financial reporting.

In the following table there are some suggestions for other performance measures.

	Possible Performance Measures
Consumers	Number of complaints, time taken to answer query, what are the numbers and types of consumers?
Results	Output quantity, costs per period
Process	End-to-end time of process (and sub-processes), set-up times, amount of errors picked up in the process, amount of scrap and rework, equipment availability/downtime, number of suggestions for improvement, number of suggestions implemented
Inputs	Errors in receivables (different types) and quantities
Suppliers	Correctness of invoices, time to answer inquiries, on-time deliveries

Learning Summary

- 2F can be used to list either the different performance measures or the processes used to obtain them

- Figures or numbers from performance measurement provide a better basis for decisions than "gut feel"

- Real-world numbers contain random fluctuations that hide possible signals for action, which are hidden by totals and averages

- Process behaviour charts provide a process to transform performance measurements into system or process knowledge

- Process behaviour charts reveal whether measures are safe to use as a basis for prediction and contain action signals, and, objectively, whether changes really are improvements

- The five types of measures offer a more complete picture of performance than financial figures alone

Activity

What are your performance measurements? What processes do you use to understand what they are telling you about what is happening?

Chapter 16 - Processes for Understanding Consumers & Context

Chapter Gist

Consumer Feedback

Strategic leadership reviews of the progress that an organisation is making towards its aims must be informed by knowledge about the consumer. Knowledge from the sales force and consumer-facing staff in particular must be part of this.

Knowledge of External Context or Environment

There is a wide range of external influences on an organisation.

Consumer Feedback

As long ago as 1997, consultancy KMPG reported that the tendency in marketing had moved to recording what people actually did. Buying "intentions" as revealed by surveys had not proved a reliable indicator.

At the very basic level, what knowledge do you have about what your consumers do? What are their buying patterns, or the equivalent, in terms of the product or service mix, geographical patterns, time of the day, different purchasing methods – such as the Internet, and so on? Recording this knowledge and understanding how it is changing with time, where possible in a process behaviour chart, will be important. This knowledge needs to be collected and provided for consideration so that strategic decisions are properly informed.

Due weight must be given to the knowledge developed by sales and consumer-facing staff, who are often in the best position to understand consumers. As is frequently said in sales, people buy from people. Relationships developed should lead to an in-depth understanding of consumers that must also inform strategic decisions.

In the era of best value, the writer has observed a tendency in the public sector for much gathering of knowledge about consumers. Regrettably too often no processes exist to use this knowledge to drive strategic decision making, change, improvement and innovation, or service delivery. Central government bears heavy responsibility for this through the use of diktat and by setting a poor example.

The actual "voice" of the consumer is received from incoming communications of all types and by surveying consumers through interviews and focus groups. Space does not permit a detailed treatment of this here but there are techniques to handle verbal, qualitative information. Possibly language processing or even the academic technique of grounded theory might be used.

Knowledge of External Context or Environment

The external operating environment includes a range of influences, for example the marketplace, economy, politics and the legislature, and environmental factors such as climate change. Currently, much of this may be taken in only informally, possibly only subconsciously.

A process is required to make available as complete a picture as possible of the external environment, to be used when making strategic decisions. This process can draw on information from industry associations, universities, government departments and agencies, and international organisations

Learning Summary

- Processes must exist to provide knowledge about the consumer to inform strategic decisions

- The sales force and consumer-facing staff are in a good position to provide this knowledge

- Knowledge about a wide range of external influences on an organisation must be available when strategic decisions are taken

Activity

What processes exist to use performance measurements and other consumer feedback to obtain knowledge that will support strategic leadership processes? What are the parallel processes that deal with the external context or environment?

Chapter 17 – Strategic Leadership Processes

> ## Chapter Gist
>
> ### Strategic Leadership Processes: Wisdom
>
> These processes review what is actually happening, including the voice of the consumer, against the stated aims. The results of the review then need to be understood in order to make wise choices.
>
> ### Statement of Aims
>
> Stating the organisation's aims helps clarify thinking as well as provide direction. A useful three-part statement of aims for an organisation comprises its purpose, vision and values.
>
> ### Informal Strategic Leadership Processes
>
> Strategic leadership processes may be formal or informal, depending perhaps on the size and type of business or organisation. The effectiveness of these processes should be reviewed from time to time.
>
> ### Leading the System
>
> 2F may help develop the ability in leaders to think of the organisation as a system, and to understand that outcomes result from the entire organisation working together.

Strategic Leadership Processes

At the beginning of this book, the lack of success in achieving change was attributed partly to the lack of effective leadership. It was suggested that processes might help a wider range of leaders succeed with change.

The main recurring strategic leadership process is to review where the organisation is at any given time compared to its aims. This must be based on a balanced review of a range of performance measures from across the business. Some of the underlying data will be quantitative, numerical, and some of it may be qualitative. What is important is that this counterbalances the "gut feel" tendency so that wise choices are made. Particularly important in this is to consider whatever represents the voice of the consumer.

A ship's voyage may act as a helpful metaphor here. The overall strategic goal may be to travel from Southampton to New York. A certain course will be plotted across the Atlantic depending on the time of year and the weather forecast. Once the voyage has started, small corrections will be necessary to accommodate tides and winds, which will be part of the primary process. However, should a severe storm or an iceberg be encountered, the captain may order a significant change of course. If for some reason New York becomes closed to shipping, a strategic decision may be taken, by the captain in collaboration with the owners, to go Boston.

Back in an organisation, the review process may determine that changes or a "course correction" are necessary. The required change would be passed to the relevant processes for designing and redesigning the system.

In the writer's experience, policy making in the public sector is equivalent to strategic leadership processes. This is a strength, but one could wish for a greater use of evidence-based policy making as its absence can lead to layers of policy and legislation that increase waste.

Statement of Aims

The assumption is that the aim or goal for the business or organisation is written down. If it is not, it helps to use a statement of aims that comprises three parts: the purpose (as covered in Chapter 6), a vision and values.

The process of writing down the aims clarifies thinking. Actually, generating a statement of aims in a group can be a powerful way to align people in the business or organisation to their goal. Peter Scholtes has written usefully on purpose, vision and values in *The Leader's Handbook*.

Inspirational vision in particular is central to leadership. Unfortunately space and the scope of this book do not allow much room for further discussion. Read around the subject of vision yourself, for as Peter Senge says in *The Fifth Discipline*: "A shared vision is... a force in people's hearts", satisfying "their desire to be connected in an important undertaking".

The aims themselves should be regularly checked in the light of knowledge about consumer wants and needs and the whole external operating environment. Clearly if the external goalposts move, the aim must change and so must the organisation.

Informal Strategic Leadership Processes

It should be stated here that in some organisations, probably small and medium-sized businesses, strategic leadership processes as such are informal. This is fine.

How do you recognise them? Well, such processes may take place during quiet moments, perhaps with a coffee or your favourite tipple, perhaps during a walk in the hills. They may be in the form of conversations with friends, family, staff or colleagues. The point is to recognise that you are working out how you are doing and what, if anything, needs to be changed.

At these times, you are more in *Entrepreneur* personality, as Michael Gerber calls it in *The E Myth Revisited*. This book is a useful read for all small and medium-sized business owners and managers.

If the goal has changed or a course correction is required, Chapter 19 on Change Management, gives one example of a process that a leader of change could use.

Leading the System

Leadership, whether by an individual or a group, involves aspects of behaviour and abilities. 2F may help develop the ability in leaders to think of the organisation as a system. This means understanding that outcomes are the result of all elements and aspects of the organisation working together. Michael Simmons in *New Leadership for Women and Men* describes this as: "Working to understand the whole situation..." The writer has heard Dr Myron Tribus describe what leaders do as: "work on the system to continually improve it" with everyone's help.

As well as being a systemic issue, leadership is about creating an environment that is both stimulating and in which risks can be taken, providing the consumer is not affected. In the end, being a genuine human being is probably the most important way any leader can create that environment.

Learning Summary

- Strategic leadership processes review progress against the aim and test the validity of that aim

- A useful format for a statement of aims comprises purpose, vision and values

- Strategic leadership processes may be formal or informal

- 2F may help leaders to understand organisations as systems

- Read the books with "leadership" in the title in Resources, plus the *Tao Te Ching*

Activity

What are your strategic leadership processes? What is your statement of aims?

Chapter 18 – Processes to Design & Redesign the System

Chapter Gist

The What! Changing the System

Putting strategic decisions into practice requires processes. These may range from one-off cross-functional teams or special design functions that bring in people from across the organisation. The lack of attention to this area makes change ineffective.

Innovative Environment

Leadership is required for an innovative environment that is safe and stimulating. Fear is not supportive of innovation. Leadership may have to develop an inspiring vision to raise the emotional level to stimulate new ideas. Ongoing waste elimination and continual improvement can contribute to an environment where new ideas thrive.

The What! Changing the System

We now move on to "the what and the how" of designing or redesigning specific changes to the whole system including products, services and processes.

How will these be created? What processes are in place?

On new projects, it can be valuable to involve as many people as possible from across the organisation. In smaller organisations, possibly a cross-functional team will be assembled each time for one particular design or redesign project. Even where there are special design functions or departments, seconding people from the primary and support processes can lead to better products, services or processes. The members of such teams could be used as project leaders and trainers when putting the change into practice.

Frequently, insufficient care and effort are invested in planning, designing and putting new services or processes into practice. Chapter 19 gives some guidance on the latter. At worst, and not only in the public sector, the whole of this part of 2F and the next is little more than a communication exercise or a diktat – "just do it!" Without care, thought and much detailed work at this stage, it is back to "reorganising deckchairs on the Titanic".

Having arrived at a new product, service or process, try it out on a small-scale pilot or prototype test. The learning from this should ensure a better result when put into practice on a large scale.

An alternative is to put in place processes that commission consultants, contractors or partners to provide original input. The problem here of course is the danger of the "not invented here" syndrome, the difficulty of acceptance of new ideas from outside. Equally there is the problem of losing access to outsiders' expertise once the project has finished.

Innovative Environment

Necessity is the mother of invention, as the saying goes. However, it is possibly easier to be open to new ideas when starting a new business or process because the emotional energy is higher. It is natural to think about what the consumers want and need and, more importantly, are willing to pay for when not having to meet day-to-day demands.

A useful starting point for a new product or service is to look at consumer and market research data, which is collected when trying to understand consumers and the external context. The inspiring vision talked of in Chapter 19 may need to be generated by leadership to make "Necessity..." more exciting in established organisations!

The individual businessperson, micro or small business may, on the other hand, rely on their own creativity. The challenge is to make the space and time available whilst running the business. Perhaps creative ideas can be captured, however weird, in a **New Ideas** file? This could also contain articles or news items. Time still has to be made to look at the file, of course.

Creating new products, services or processes will require the right environment. We are back to Maslow again! The leadership has a great responsibility to encourage a safe but stimulating environment. Do not expect creativity and innovation in an environment of fear – ingenuity will only be used to avoid the pain!

Care should be taken not to overemphasise competition. "Losers" may not support "winning" designs nor feel inclined to point out possible vulner-abilities.

As discussed below in Chapter 19, the environment and skills required for waste elimination and continual improvement should also stimulate innovation. Thus waste elimination and continual improvement might be considered essential processes to support innovation.

Learning Summary

- Processes are required for designing or redesigning new products, services or processes

- Bringing in people from primary and support processes can lead to better designs and putting them in place more successfully

- A safe but stimulating environment is required in which to design new products, services or processes

- Do not expect creativity and innovation in an environment of fear

Activity

What processes do you have to design and redesign the system? How do you create an environment that stimulates creativity and innovation?

Chapter 19 – Change Management Processes

> ## Chapter Gist
>
> ### Change Processes
>
> Communication-only change processes will not produce sustainable change. Research suggests that change, particularly large-scale change, follows a process.
>
> ### Change: Rational or Emotional?
>
> Often, people do not resist change; they resist BEING changed. According to research, people deal with change in an emotional rather than a rational, logical way. In the grieving cycle, you may recognise your own responses to change.
>
> ### Big Change + Smaller Change
>
> The frequent smaller changes that are part of continual improvement help to establish an environment and skills from which innovation, large-scale change, can benefit.
>
> ### Making Big Change Easier
>
> When large-scale change is necessary, processes such as the eight-step one described go beyond the idea that communication alone sustains the change.

The material in this chapter on the Kotter 8-Step Change Process is from *The Heart of Change* and is used by kind permission of Harvard Business School Press.

Change Processes

Does your business or organisation have a proven process that produces sustainable change? Research by Professor John Kotter seems to show that successful change, particularly large-scale change, follows a process. Communication alone as a process will not produce sustainable change.

Making changes, just like anything else in organisations, is a set of processes. These may be thought of as projects because there are specific goals, timescales and amounts of resource allocated. However, hopefully eventually, and after doing what is proposed in this book, change will become part of the way you do business. Therefore, even though each change or improvement project may be different, the way the organisation goes about making changes should follow a pattern that itself is continually improved. Thus it is a process.

Change: Rational or Emotional?

Often, people do not resist change; they resist *being* changed.

According to John Kotter and Dan Cohen, in *The Heart of Change*, the biggest mistake made in thinking about change is believing that people can deal with it in a logical, rational way. The change process is rarely **analysis-think-change**. Do read this excellent book.

Kotter's research shows that successful change occurs almost always when leaders understand that change is an emotional process. In emotional change, the process is usually **see-feel-change**.

The Grieving Cycle (see Part 5) perhaps explains the stages that people go through when experiencing change, particularly large-scale change. A whole range of emotions is involved in grieving and letting go. Clearly it will not work to just "communicate", or announce, the change and run for the hills, which is often management's normal behaviour in these situations!

Big Change + Smaller Change

The section on quality in Part 5 suggests that there is a Quality Spectrum: Maintain Standards ➔ Continual Improvement ➔ Innovation.

Maintain standards means no change; continual improvement means ongoing, small changes; and innovation means less frequent, large changes.

This book proposes that if people are encouraged and expected to carry out continual improvement while also maintaining standards, openness to change will tend to become part of the "way you do business". Continual improvement, or smaller changes, requires a supportive environment and skills. This can, and should be, change from the bottom up. These smaller changes are *their* changes!

Suggestion schemes are a way of managing this; they also require processes to try out, implement and standardise many small improvements. The environment and knowledge created by many small changes should stimulate innovation and make bigger changes both easier and more frequent.

Making Big Change Easier

Well, it is not always going to be easy. People's responses will vary because it is an emotional process. When it comes to putting in place innovative or larger changes, a process is required to help people make those changes.

Kotter summarises his research in an eight-step process, all of which is necessary to achieve successful, enduring change. These steps are restated as:

1. Get Attention, Raise Awareness

    Understand the whole situation and then generate a feeling of urgency for change by some dramatically visible sign of the need for change. Try to reduce the complacency, fear and anger that prevent change.

2. Create a Steering Team

    Assemble an effective steering team to lead the change effort, choosing people who have the right characteristics and authority. They will need to behave with enthusiasm, trust and emotional commitment; setting a good example or "walking the talk".

3. Blend an Inspiring Vision

    Create an inspiring vision to focus the change, and to make the change by using more than just the usual analysis, plans and budgets. The steering team needs to develop effective strategies to realise the inspiring vision.

4. Honestly Convey the Inspiring Vision

    This requires two-way communication where listening is particularly important. Acknowledge the uncomfortable feelings caused by change. Convey the message clearly, concisely and visually. Management need to be seen to set an example – to "walk the talk". Oh yes, and cut out the hype!

5.   Give Permission and Remove Roadblocks

Release new behaviours by removing organisational and emotional barriers, like bureaucracy. Use Herzberg's non-financial motivators, such as recognition for those who embrace the vision and new strategies. Focus development reviews on how people are contributing to the change.

6.   Quick Wins – Pick Low Hanging Fruit

Build momentum by running a few small projects initially that can produce short-term results and reinforce the change. These provide feedback to the leaders and encouragement to those working on the change.

7.   Maintain Momentum

Programme a continuous succession of projects that reinforce the change. Share success stories. Look for measures or signs in behaviours and language to assess whether change is permanent. Keep on conveying that vision. Seize every opportunity imaginatively to enable people to see the change working.

8.   Sustain the New Way

One of the most visible ways to sustain a change is to promote only those who have wholeheartedly embraced the change and got results.

Induction and training must be changed to ensure that new staff and management understand the new way. Remember how much learning everyone in the organisation has done to get to where they are today.

Nearly the most important long-term thing to do is to make sure that all of those at the highest level in the organisation are all committed to the change. For example, when recruiting new members to the Board of Directors in the private sector, make sure the selection process reinforces the new way. This is particularly important in the case of the chief executives or their equivalent. You do not want "new brooms" to sweep away all that hard-won learning. Consider what special induction process they might need.

Even after three highly successful years operating in a new and better way, CEO Rob Rodin reported that he was asked: "Are we still doing this stuff?" It might take ten years or more before large-scale change is fully embedded in an organisational culture. It may take longer depending on the life or development cycle of products and services. Rodin's book *Free, Perfect and Now* is well worth reading to follow an organisational transformation journey.

Learning Summary

- A process involving more than just communication is required for sustainable change

- People deal with change in an emotional way, not a rational, logical way

- In the grieving cycle, perhaps you can recognise the feelings you experience with forced change

- An environment that encourages continual improvement provides people with the opportunity to get used to change and to making their own changes

- This environment and the knowledge generated is helpful to stimulating innovation and large-scale change

- Use the eight-step process for sustainable large-scale change

Activity

Rate your leadership of change: 1=Often 2=Seldom 3=Never. Do you:

1. [ ] Successfully and sustainably implement significant or transformational change
2. [ ] Use a process for significant or transformational change
3. [ ] Understand and generate a feeling of urgency for change
4. [ ] Reduce the complacency, fear and anger that prevent change
5. [ ] Assemble an effective steering team to lead the change effort
6. [ ] Select a steering team that has the right characteristics and authority
7. [ ] Behave with trust and emotional commitment
8. [ ] Change using more than just the usual analytical and financial plans and budgeting
9. [ ] Create an inspiring vision to direct change
10. [ ] Lead a steering team that develops effective strategies to realise an inspiring vision
11. [ ] Communicate the direction of change clearly, credibly and sincerely
12. [ ] Encourage genuine emotional commitment that is evident in the way people act
13. [ ] Use a wide range of actions to clear and overcome confusion and distrust
14. [ ] Remove barriers that block those who support the vision and strategies
15. [ ] Release new behaviours by removing organisational and emotional barriers
16. [ ] Generate quick wins
17. [ ] Build momentum
18. [ ] Make successes visible, unambiguous and relevant to what people care about
19. [ ] Help create wave after wave of change that makes the vision reality
20. [ ] Maintain the urgency until change is sustained
21. [ ] Address difficult issues, transformational issues and, particularly, emotional issues
22. [ ] Maintain energy by eliminating needless work
23. [ ] Change group or organisational practices to encourage new behaviours
24. [ ] Enhance new norms and values using induction, promotions and emotion

What does this tell you about the way you lead change?

Based on *The Heart of Change* by John P. Kotter and Dan S. Cohen

---

Activity

Where do you see opportunities to improve your change management?

PART 4
ARE YOU READY?

What do you think? Hopefully, if you have not already been using it, you are ready to try using 2F for your business or organisation. To conclude, here are some tips on how to proceed next as well as some words of caution.

Chapter 20 – What Next? Using 2F

Chapter Gist

Questions, Questions

The questions raised up to this point should have set you off towards a better future. Some tips are suggested to help you get going.

Process Mapping

Describe your processes or activities in a deployment flowchart.

Process Behaviour Charting

Put your numbers, figures or data in graphical form to increase knowledge and understanding of all aspects of your system.

Questions, Questions

Just asking all the questions, and finding the answers, that it will have taken to get to this point should have started you on the road to a better future. You may even be very excited. It will also be mind-boggling. Here are some tips that might help.

1. Compile a business system manual in a form that works for you. If you go to www.pictureyourbusiness.co.uk, you will find an A4 template for 2F in Microsoft® Word

2. Use 2F both as a framework for all the processes at all levels in your business or organisation and as a new organisation chart showing process owners and team leaders

3. To save your sanity and make change happen, you will need not only to plan but also to prioritise

4. You will need to allocate resources, that is PEOPLE, MONEY and TIME. Sorry to shout, but it really will not happen unless you stop doing some of the things that you currently do. Be brave!

5. It may be necessary to bring in some additional help and expertise

6. The next major step is to go into more detail in each of the seven process areas by mapping each of the processes (see more about process mapping below)

7. Start to record performance measurements in process behaviour charts (see below)

8. Build in regular process checks to check your progress

9. If a quality or performance problem is a high priority, it may pay to start with the particular processes, product and services involved, then continually improve and use SAPDo with 2F providing knowledge of the whole situation for a particular process

Process Mapping

Process mapping is a graphical method of recording and analysing work or business processes as a basis for ongoing improvement.

Deployment flowcharting is a particularly powerful form of flowchart. It includes all the people or departments that are involved in the process, showing who does what before whom. It also has an important role in helping to achieve change, because it forces everyone to face up to what is really happening in the organisation. Usually it uncovers much complexity and confusion. Below is a simple example.

You can find out how to set about mapping processes using the deployment flowchart in *The Gist of Process Mapping* (Clark, 2005).

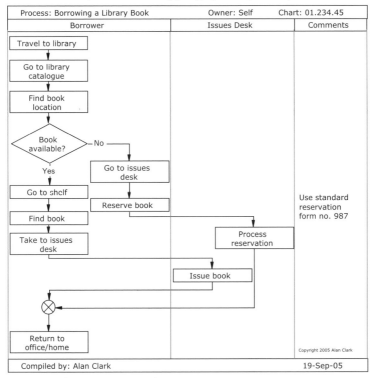

Process: Borrowing a Library Book	Owner: Self	Chart: 01.234.45
Borrower	Issues Desk	Comments

Process Behaviour Charting (PBC)

This is a reminder to use time-series graphs in PBC format to record and analyse data, which was mentioned in Chapter 15. These extract more knowledge from performance measures. PBC is very important in planning things to do next. Practise with figures you use every day.

Start by collecting, say, the last two years' monthly data of existing performance measures from your system. Initially just put them on simple graphs against the data. Look for patterns in the graphs and try to link them to the actual events in the process or its environment. Does a link increase your knowledge and understanding of the process?

To learn how to turn these graphs into PBCs, you could use Don Wheeler's book *Understanding Variation*.

Activity

In this space, write down in priority order the processes from the seven main areas that you have identified above and then process map each one. Start your list with the primary processes or areas where you have identified problems already.

Chapter 21 – Health Warning

Nothing is perfect, including 2F, so here are some things to watch out for:

- Do not bet the ranch! Which means be careful and do not jump straight in feet first. Draft 2F for your organisation in rough. Think about it. Discuss it or better still fill it out with the people in your business. Speak to friends or a trusted business advisor.

- There is no substitute for the brain, as Deming once sagely observed. 2F is there to aid thinking, not replace it completely. The questions raised by 2F will be as important as putting it into practice.

- Do not be constrained by the boxes. If in your industry or sector there is a unique process area, which, say, overlaps the seven areas above, then put it in.

- Even the line between primary processes and outcomes is blurred. Suppose your business is a restaurant or you cater for dinner parties. Is your outcome just delivering the food to the table, the great conversation after the meal or the warm glow afterwards felt by all the diners? It is your choice, hopefully, informed by your consumers.

- Managers at all levels, supervisors and team leaders need to adopt mindsets and behaviours that create and endorse the 2F diagram, otherwise gains will be lost.

- Remember that arbitrary numerical targets only distort the system, achieving one thing usually at the expense of others. A methodical approach to change is required, based upon knowledge of the system, ideally using process behaviour charts.

Activity

Some interesting questions:

1. What have you learned about your business?

2. In what way can you see that you can do a better job for the consumer of your outcomes?

3. What have you learned about yourself?

4. What have you learned about your consumers?

5. What are you going to do?

6. What are you going to do more of that you are already doing?

7. What are you going to stop doing?

Chapter 22 – Bottom Line

Using the 2F diagram brings the following advantages:

- Change is built into the way you do business
- The focus is on how value can be added for the consumer
- Continual improvement and innovation of products, services and processes are achieved alongside SAPDo
- An organisational environment that stimulates innovation is created

Bottom, Bottom Line

- Better responsiveness
- More effective and sustainable change
- Less waste
- Happy stakeholders = EXTRAORDINARY BUSINESS

Why wait?

Start now!

Have fun! ☺

f you would like to offer some feedback, please email:
nfo@pictureyourbusiness.co.uk

PART 5
RESOURCES

The Grieving Cycle

The writer first came across the grieving cycle when presented by Minnesota-based psychologist Anna Maravelas at a BDA Transformation Forum in the 1990s. It immediately struck a chord and has proved useful in understanding people's reaction to change.

Elizabeth Kübler-Ross in *On Death and Dying* reported the emotional stages that people go through when dealing with tragic news. People appeared to go through a roller coaster of emotions including shock, denial, bargaining, anger, sadness, before reaching acceptance.

William Bridges explored his own experiences in *Transitions: Making Sense of Life's Changes*. Bridges suggests that there are three stages in change: Endings, the Neutral Zone and the New Beginning.

What was interesting was how Maravelas overlaid the roller coaster of emotions resulting from change with Bridges' three zones. Strangely enough, hearing the news of change evokes feelings of shock that really only mark the beginning of the endings zone. Acceptance is at the low point reached in the middle of the neutral zone. Only then are people facing change ready to listen in detail to what the new situation might mean and start to prepare for the new beginnings. It takes time for feelings to return to near normal levels.

Maravelas struck a particular chord, noting that during the endings zone you will hear people telling "war stories" over and over. "Do you remember when we worked through the weekend to finish that report?" "I remember when the legislation changed, we had to... on the computer system."

Have you noticed how some management vanish after change has been announced? They fail to realise that, if they really want to change to move forward, they have work to do and responsibilities to their team. During endings, managers can help people through change by recognising their difficulties. They can acknowledge them by saying, and meaning, things like:

"Thank you, you did a good job."

"This is not your fault."

"This is hard isn't it?"

This last one is important because too often there is the temptation to minimise, just like our mothers did: "Don't worry, it'll be alright."

Being there for people will help during the neutral zone when there will be feelings of emptiness, of loss.

Bridges suggests that perhaps other people might be better at noticing when you enter new beginnings. That is when you really have accepted change and are ready to think about how to get to the end result.

Instead of attempting to reach the final result in one mighty bound, and beating yourself up when you fail, try an alternative. Bridges suggests that working through four stages is more helpful: stop preparing and get going; imagine what it would be like when you reach your goal; take it step by step; and treat your progress towards your goal as a learning process.

Message to managers: "change IS an emotional process, not a switch." Ignoring people's emotions, particularly your own, helps nobody. Accepting and working with this notion doesn't make it less painful. However, it should help people move on, including you.

Quality

You know what quality is. Everyone carries with them their own idea of quality. Dr William Glasser, in *Choice Theory*, says that since birth everyone develops their own idea of a "quality world".

Quality is a basic human value. Everyone, given the chance, wants to do a good job or be part of a successful enterprise.

Robert Pirsig seems to agree. The author of *Zen and the Art of Motorcycle Maintenance: An Inquiry into Values* rejects the ancient Greek philosopher's idea that subject–object is the basic human value. When you touch a hot surface, you do not think: "Hmm, this is hot and is hurting me, therefore I will remove my hand." No. It is more like "Ouch!" followed instantaneously by a reflex action of the body withdrawing the hand. The body knows this is a non-quality experience!

Quality is also the business word for truth, according to Charles Handy in *The Age of Unreason*. Like university researchers searching for knowledge, organisations should be searching for the truth about the operating environment and hidden consumer needs. This extends to delivering the products and services that you say you will.

The Chartered Quality Institute defines quality as fitness for purpose or how closely products and services meet requirements or expectations.

Considering the wide range that quality can take, Professor Noriaki Kano used psychological theory to propose three types of quality:

- Must-be-quality: that people expect, but will not tell you about

- Normal quality: where more is better, and people will tell you about

- Exciting quality: that people really want when they see it because it meets some unfulfilled need, but could not have told you about because they were unaware of it

Perhaps from this you can see that, at the most fundamental human level, the delivery process must be capable of delivering what we say it will. That is to say, it is fit for purpose. Masaaki Imai in *Gamba Kaizen* calls this maintaining standards. There is a need for continual improvement. There is also an ongoing opportunity for exceeding consumers' expectations, in other words innovating. What is interesting is that things become familiar and expectations are always rising. What was exciting quality will, over time, become normal quality and ultimately must-be-quality.

Back to Pirsig again, this time to *Lila: An Inquiry into Morals* where he states that there are two types of quality, static and dynamic, and we need both. Static quality is the equivalent of maintaining standards or must-be-quality. Dynamic quality could apply to both continual improvement and innovation.

Inspecting quality in products and services is expensive and not foolproof. Try checking your own written work, particularly when you have done it in a hurry. It is too easy to miss your own errors. Modern quality management aims for processes that are "capable", which means that, when operating normally, they can maintain standards or deliver must-be-quality without problems.

So the issue is not understanding what quality is; everyone knows instinctively what it is, and expectations of quality are always rising. No. The challenge is the delivery of quality, making it part of the way we do business and equal with other aspects of the business of delivering products and services.

As the writer once heard Hal Mather say in a seminar: "Customers are paying to be satisfied." What you should aim for is customer delight. Stephen Covey suggests that there is something beyond even customer delight, namely customer *insistence*. In terms of the success of any organisation, providing products and services that consumers insist on has got to be on the right track.

Apparently, more than half of consumers who say they are satisfied are still liable to defect to another supplier. Some aspect is not right and therefore the supplier is vulnerable.

So everyone, including our consumers, knows what quality is for them. We need to be able to have a capable way of consistently delivering it. Since expectations are always rising, we need to continually improve our products or services. If we really want to stay ahead of the game, we must innovate.

Truly adopting a wide vision of quality will therefore literally pay dividends.

Success, even survival, ultimately depends upon quality being a fundamental value in organisations. This should not be a problem since, as Glasser and Pirsig suggest, it is the fundamental human value. The problem is usually this: the working environment too often does not show that it values quality, and places the emphasis on profit, targets or management ego. So the issue is the system, not the people. Who is responsible for the system...?

Continual Improvement & SAPDo

It seems appropriate to say more about continual improvement. From the above, we can see what might be called a Quality Spectrum: Maintain Standards ➜ Continual Improvement ➜ Innovation.

Continual Improvement (CI) is a fundamentally different way of managing an organisation. It focuses on work as processes, particularly those that add value for the consumer, and strives for ongoing evidence-based improvement (using measurement) of consumer-perceived quality of the outcomes. It has much in common with lean management and ideally would be used alongside it. Starting with CI, you might end up doing lean management too.

The CI approach replaces conventional problem solving and has a different starting point, using visual management tools to study the problem, identify root causes and change the process or system. There is a wide range of these visual management tools, two of the most important being the deployment flowchart and the process behaviour charts (or Shewhart Charts) – graphical ways of analysing data (see Chapters 15 and 20).

Ultimately, CI moves the organisation away from a reactive to a proactive stance, driving up quality and performance by looking at the root causes of problems. It will at the same time lead to a reduction in waste.

It is *only* CI when a methodical approach is taken that uses the Study-Act-Plan-Do (SAPDo) learning spiral (see Figure 5). To many, this may be familiar as the PDSA cycle, Deming Wheel or even Plan-Do-Check-Act (PDCA).

Figure 5

This book makes the point that almost all of the time CI is used to solve a problem in, or to improve an existing system. The first thing that must be done is to understand the whole situation. It makes more sense, therefore, to refer to it in the order that you would normally start at "Study". Although PDCA is widely used and is in ISO 9000:2000, "Check" sounds superficial compared with "Study" and in some places can mean just tick the box.

History: 2F Origins

The 2F diagram has its immediate roots in the flow diagram used by W Edwards Deming in summer 1950 in Japan. Indeed he claims that it was this flow diagram and not the use of process behaviour charts (also known as Statistical Process Control) that was the spark that ignited Japan's posst-War economic revolution. The flow diagram of production viewed as a system has all the elements of a classic feedback model. That this diagram was on page 4 of his seminal book *Out of the Crisis* shows the importance he placed on it.

One might speculate that the origin of Deming's flow diagram was linked both to Deming's own first degree in electrical engineering and also to the field of cybernetics, which was leading-edge thinking during and after the Second World War. More likely, it was an amplification of a three-step cycle, specification, production, inspection, which Walter Shewhart, Deming's mentor and collaborator, describes in *Statistical Method from the Viewpoint of Quality Control* (1939). Deming's flow diagram is his Plan-Do-Study-Act (PDSA) cycle running anticlockwise (see Chapter 3).

In 1997 Dr Myron Tribus presented Elaine Torres' interpretation of Deming's flow diagram for a school in a paper to the annual UK Deming Forum. This was later generalised for all organisations by Terry Peterson. He included leadership processes in the feedback loop; these processes now provide a link through to ISO 9000 and Integrated Management Systems. In some circles it is still known as the Torres-Peterson diagram. Gari Jones of DVLA and consultant Michael Simmons further refined it. Simmons described the flow path as the operational level and the feedback path as the strategic level. It is critical for management at every level to realise that strategic leadership is a set of processes for which *they* are responsible. At a meeting in December 2005 of the Deming Special Interest Group (in what is now the Chartered Quality Institute), Simmons showed how the basic structure of the 2F diagram could be used for strategy mapping and deployment.

The writer has amplified the area of performance measures to explicitly include data from suppliers, inputs, process, results and consumer feedback. The data in these boxes tells us how well we are doing. Process behaviour (or Shewhart control) charts should be used to process data into knowledge and understanding. The writer has also added indications to show cost, waste, profit and morale and motivation as outcomes of the system. Motivation as an outcome refers back to Senge's conclusion (see

Chapter 2) that the system or structure influences behaviour. Finally, change management has been positioned to show that it takes the outcomes of system design and redesign and puts them into practice across the whole organisation.

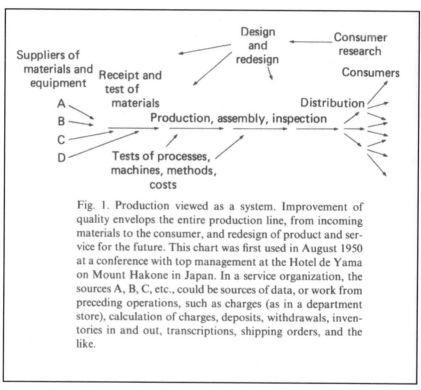

Fig. 1. Production viewed as a system. Improvement of quality envelops the entire production line, from incoming materials to the consumer, and redesign of product and service for the future. This chart was first used in August 1950 at a conference with top management at the Hotel de Yama on Mount Hakone in Japan. In a service organization, the sources A, B, C, etc., could be sources of data, or work from preceding operations, such as charges (as in a department store), calculation of charges, deposits, withdrawals, inventories in and out, transcriptions, shipping orders, and the like.

Management: Lean or Mean?

Nothing is new, including lean management, as a passage in *The Portsmouth Block Mills* by Jonathan Coad illustrates. He describes the rebuilding of two Royal Naval Dockyards between 1760 and 1800. He says efforts were made to replan the dockyards to reduce unnecessary journeys, locating storehouses near where their contents were needed and siting the enormous roperies to cause least obstruction. This was all good "lean" practice.

Lean management is more than one of the current catchphrases; it is a different way of managing businesses and organisations. It is the generic name given to the form of management, otherwise known as the Toyota Production System, which has taken Toyota to a leading position both in output growth and profitability in the global automotive industry. The overall focus is one of *delivering value* to the customers or consumers. The significance of Toyota's progress using the system is that it prospers whilst its major competitors are struggling to survive under the same global economic conditions. It even profitably manufactures vehicles in the USA where local high-volume competitors struggle.

"That's all well and good," you might say, "but our business does not make vehicles." The principles of lean management are in fact applicable to any sector and any type of organisation. It is built upon two pillars.

Twin Pillars of Lean

- Elimination of all non-value-adding wastes
- Respect for people

The suite of management tools and techniques that are part of lean management has beguiled many people over the years into thinking that is all there is to it. Possibly due in part to Toyota protecting its competitive advantage, the true breadth of lean management and the importance of *respect for people* have been underestimated.

Elimination of all non-value-adding wastes becomes a mindset that is served by the many tools and techniques. Combining the two pillars taps into the creative contribution of all staff through suggestion schemes. There is an important change in mindset that accompanies lean management. Whilst there are hierarchies, albeit flat ones, and there is the expectation of high levels of self-discipline, this is allied to the bottom-up driven focus

127

on elimination of waste and the reduction of end-to-end process times. Waste in service sectors is hidden and especially requires the joint contribution of all of the staff and the tools and techniques.

A deep knowledge of lean and of Japanese organisations has lead Bill Waddell and Norm Bodek, in *Rebirth of American Industry,* to an interesting conclusion as to why more Western businesses have failed to follow Toyota's success.

They believe it is Return on Investment (ROI)-driven accounting that is the root cause for the failure to stick with lean management in the long term. Cash accounting as ideally applied in lean management treats staff costs as fixed rather than variable costs, which allows the development of people to assume greater importance.

On the other hand, ROI puts what Waddell and Bodek see as an unhelpful focus on a reduction in headcount apparently regardless of the effect that this has on the knowledge and skills of an organisation. How many organisations do you know that have downsized out of existence?

A lean management approach thus enhances an organisation's capability to perform and work within financial resources, whereas conventional approaches, through cost-cutting, can actually damage the ability of businesses and organisations to perform or even stay in business.

Marketing & Sales

You may well be asking where marketing and sales have gone. Well of course the activities are still there. Much like quality in the previous section, marketing is actually part of the way that you do business. In a 1997 White Paper, consultancy KPMG looked at the modern place of marketing. Their conclusion seemed to be that marketing is business – business is marketing. It should not be thought of as a door along some corridor with the sign "Marketing Department".

Marketing activities are taking place throughout the strategic level, primarily in understanding the consumers and context, and strategic leadership.

In retail sales, activities may well be taking place at the interface between primary processes and the consumer. Part of the value consumers are buying is the whole retail experience. As a consumer, you go to certain retailers because of the service, product ranges or prices. Indeed retailing, and associated restocking, may comprise the whole of the primary processes.

It can be different in business-to-business sales. In particular in the provision of one-off very large capital items or projects, the whole of 2F may be involved. Position marketing and sales activities where they increase knowledge and understanding in your system as a whole.

There are no right or wrong answers, because the purpose of 2F is to provoke questions and inquiry.

Recommended Reading

Here are some publications that have inspired me; most are cited in this book. May they inform or illuminate your journey.

William Bridges (1980) *Transitions: Making Sense of Life's Changes*, Reading MA: Perseus Books

William C Byham with Jeff Cox (1991) *Zapp! The Lightning of Empowerment*, London: Century Business

John A Carlisle and Robert C Parker (1989) *Beyond Negotiation: Redeeming Customer-Supplier Relationships*, Chichester: Wiley

Peter B Checkland (1981) *Systems Thinking, Systems Practice*, Chichester: Wiley

Alan C Clark (2005) *The Gist of Process Mapping: How to Record, Analyse and Improve Work Processes*, Evesham: Word4Word

Jonathan G Coad (2005) *The Portsmouth Block Mills: Bentham, Brunel and the Start of the Royal Navy's Industrial Revolution*, Swindon: English Heritage

Stephen R Covey (1992) *Principle Centred Leadership*, New York: Simon & Schuster

Edward L Deci and Richard M Ryan (1985) *Intrinsic Motivation and Self-Determination in Human Behavior*, New York: Plenum

W Edwards Deming (1986) *Out of the Crisis*, Cambridge MA: MIT-CAES

W Edwards Deming (1993) *The New Economics – For Industry, Government, Education*, Cambridge MA: MIT-CAES

Michael E Gerber (1995) *The E Myth Revisited*, New York: HarperBusiness

Arie de Geus (1999) *The Living Company: Growth, Learning and Longevity in Business*, London: Nicholas Brealey

William Glasser (1998) *Choice Theory: A New Psychology of Personal Freedom*, New York: HarperCollins

Charles Handy (1990) *The Age of Unreason*, London: Arrow Books

Peter Hines, Riccardo Silvi and Monica Bartolini (2002) *Lean Profit Potential*, Cardiff: Cardiff Business School, Lean Enterprise Research Centre

Masaaki Imai (1997) *Gemba Kaizen*, New York: McGraw-Hill

H Thomas Johnson (2000) *Profit Beyond Measure: Extraordinary Results Through Attention to Work and People*, London: Nicholas Brealey

Brian L Joiner (1994) *Fourth Generation Management: The New Business Consciousness*, New York: McGraw-Hill

John Kotter and Dan Cohen (2002) *The Heart of Change*, Boston MA: Harvard Business School Press

Elizabeth Kubler-Ross (1969) *On Death and Dying*, New York: Simon & Schuster/Touchstone

William J Latzko and David M Saunders (1995) *Four Days with Dr Deming*, Reading MA: Addison Wesley

Gerald J Langley, Kevin M Nolan, Thomas W Nolan, Clifford L Norman, and Lloyd P Provost (1996) *The Improvement Guide: A Practical Approach to Enhancing Organizational Performance*, San Francisco: Jossey-Bass

Jeffrey K Liker (2004) *The Toyota Way: 14 Management Principles from the World's Greatest Manufacturer*, New York: McGraw-Hill

Man-Ho Kwok, Martin Palmer and Jay Ramsay (1993) *The Illustrated Tao Te Ching*, Shaftsbury: Element

Abraham H Maslow, Deborah C Stephens and Gary Heil (1998) *Maslow on Management*, New York: Wiley

Lord Moran (1945) *The Anatomy of Courage*, London: Constable

Henry R Neave (1990) *The Deming Dimension*, Knoxville TN: SPC Press

Taiichi Ohno (1988) *Toyota Production System: Beyond Large-Scale Production*, Portland OR: Productivity Press (Translation)

Robert M Pirsig (1974) *Zen and the Art of Motorcycle Maintenance: An Inquiry into Values*, London: The Bodley Head

Robert M Pirsig (1991) *Lila: An Inquiry into Morals*, London: Bantam Press

Robert Rodin (1999) *Free, Perfect and Now: Connecting to the Three Insatiable Customer Demands: A CEO's True Story, New York*: Simon & Schuster

Peter R Scholtes (1998) *The Leader's Handbook, A Guide to Inspiring Your People and Managing the Daily Workflow*, New York: McGraw-Hill

Ricardo Semler (1993) *Maverick! The Success Story Behind the World's Most Unusual Workplace*, London: Arrow

Peter M Senge (1990) *The Fifth Discipline, The Art and Practice of the Learning Organisation*, New York: Currency Doubleday

Walter Shewhart (1939) *Statistical Method from the Viewpoint of Quality Control*, Washington DC: Graduate School of the Department of Agriculture

Walter A Shewhart (1980) *Economic Control of Quality of Manufactured Product*, Milwaukee WI: ASQC Quality Press. Originally published 1931 by D. Van Nostrand Company, Inc

Walter A Shewhart (1986) *Statistical Method from the Viewpoint of Quality Control*, New York: Dover. Originally published 1939 Washington DC: Graduate School of the Department of Agriculture

Michael Simmons (1996) *New Leadership for Women and Men: Building Inclusive Organization*, Aldershot: Gower

Bill Torbert and Associates (2004) *Action Inquiry: The Secret of Timely and Transforming Leadership*, San Francisco: Berrett-Koehler

Myron Tribus (1997) 'Schools Are Your Most Important Suppliers: How Do You Work With Them?', British Deming Association Tenth Annual Conference Programme and Information, Salisbury: British Deming Association

Kurt Vonegut (1952) *Player Piano*. New York: Delacorte Press/Seymour Lawrence

William H Waddell and Norman Bodek (2005) *Rebirth of American Industry: A Study of Lean Management*, Vancouver WA: PCS Press

Mary Walton (1989) *The Deming Management Method*, Chalford: Management Books 2000

Donald J Wheeler (1993) *Understanding Variation: The Key to Managing Chaos*, Knoxville TN: SPC Press

Donald J Wheeler (2003) *Making Sense of Data: SPC for the Service Sector*, Knoxville TN: SPC Press

Donald J Wheeler (2005) *The Six Sigma Practitioner's Guide to Data Analysis*, Knoxville TN: SPC Press

James P Womack, Daniel T Jones and Daniel Roos (1990) *The Machine that Changed the World: The Story of Lean Production*, New York: Rawson Associates

Web Links

No apologies; this is the area that is going to be out of date the quickest. Remember the first two most useful links:

www.google.co.uk Internet search engine

www.wikipedia.org Free online encyclopaedia

www.asq.org The American Society for Quality

www.bestmanufacturingpractices.com Bill Waddell

www.curiouscat.net/library John Hunter's Curious Cat Management Improvement library

www.deming.org The W Edwards Deming Institute

www.deming.org.uk Organisers of the annual UK Deming Forum

www.deming.eng.clemson.edu Deming Electronic Network (DEN); an Internet discussion list

www.dilbert.com The Dilbert office cartoon series

www.evolvingexcellence.com A great blog on Lean by the editors of Superfactory

www.leanenterprise.org.uk Lean Enterprise Research Centre at Cardiff University

www.spcpress.com The home of Donald Wheeler and SPC Press

www.superfactory.com Lots of good stuff on Lean

www.thecqi.org The Chartered Quality Institute

Index

A

Ackoff, Russell 20

adding value *see* value-adding activities

aims 90-1

assumptions 80

averages 81

B

Bridges, William 119, 120

budgets 80

C

change

    culture 61-2

    design and redesign of the system 96-7

    and emotions 100, 119-20

    increasing rate of 11-12

    and leadership 16

    sustaining 12-13

change management 26, 100, 126

    and emotions 100

    induction and training 102-3

    Kotter's eight-step process 101-2

    large and small changes 100-1

processes *cont.*

  and cost 66

  design & redesign 96-7

  performance measures 82

  primary 44-5, 48, 113

  purpose of 40

  strategic leadership 90-2

  and suppliers 52

  support 56-7

  to study profit 70

  for understanding consumers and context 86-7

products 36

  defective 27

  design 26

  new 96-7

  primary processes and 44

profit 36, 70

prototype tests 96

public sector

  and change management 26

  consumer-focused 70

  gathering information 20, 26, 86

  hidden waste 20

  policy making 90

  suppliers 52

purpose, statement of 40, 90

Q

quality 1, 121-2

    and change 100-1

    consumers and 27

    of inputs 48

R

resources 110

retail sales 129

Return On Investment (ROI) 66, 128

S

sales 86, 129

SAPDo (Study-Act-Plan-Do) learning spiral 24, 123

Scholtes, Peter 19, 74, 90-1

science, application of 18

self-actualisation 61

self-discipline 63, 127

Senge, Peter 16, 17-18, 91

service industries 20, 26, 52

service users *see* consumers

services 36

    defective 27

    design 26

    new 96-7

    and primary processes 44

Flow & Feedback
Worksheet

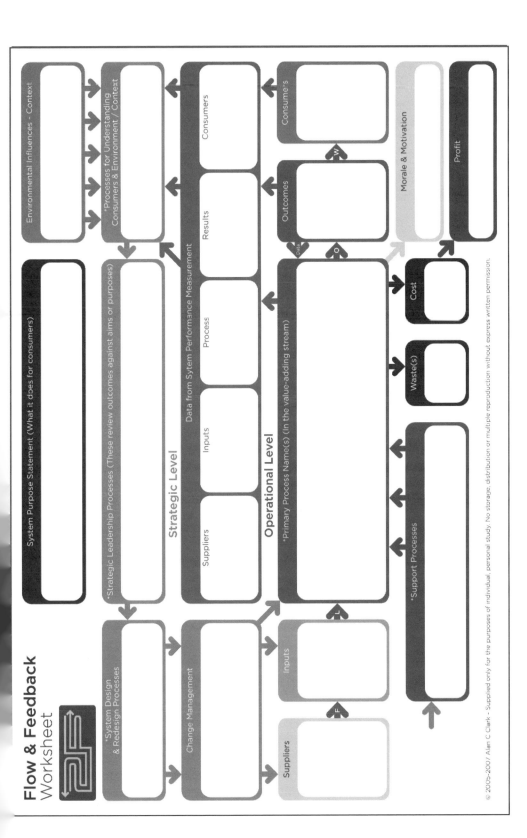

Environmental Influences – Context

*Processes for Understanding Consumers & Environment / Context

Consumers

Results

Consumers

Outcomes

Morale & Motivation

Profit

System Purpose Statement (What it does for consumers)

*Strategic Leadership Processes (These review outcomes against aims or purposes)

Data from System Performance Measurement

Strategic Level

Suppliers | Inputs | Process | Results | Consumers

Operational Level

*Primary Process Name(s) (in the value-adding stream)

Cost

Waste(s)

*System Design & Redesign Processes

Change Management

Inputs

Suppliers

*Support Processes

Your notes

Flow & Feedback
Worksheet

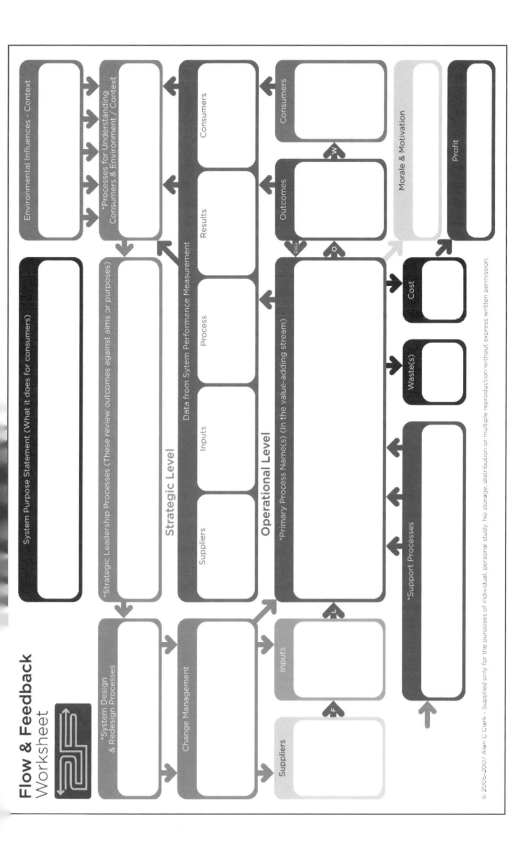

Environmental Influences - Context

*Processes for Understanding Consumers & Environment / Context

System Purpose Statement (What it does for consumers)

*Strategic Leadership Processes (These review outcomes against aims or purposes)

Strategic Level

Data from System Performance Measurement

| Suppliers | Inputs | Process | Results | Consumers |

Operational Level

*Primary Process Name(s) (In the value-adding stream)

Consumers

Outcomes

Morale & Motivation

Profit

Cost

Waste(s)

*System Design & Redesign Processes

Change Management

Inputs

Suppliers

*Support Processes

Your notes

Flow & Feedback
Worksheet

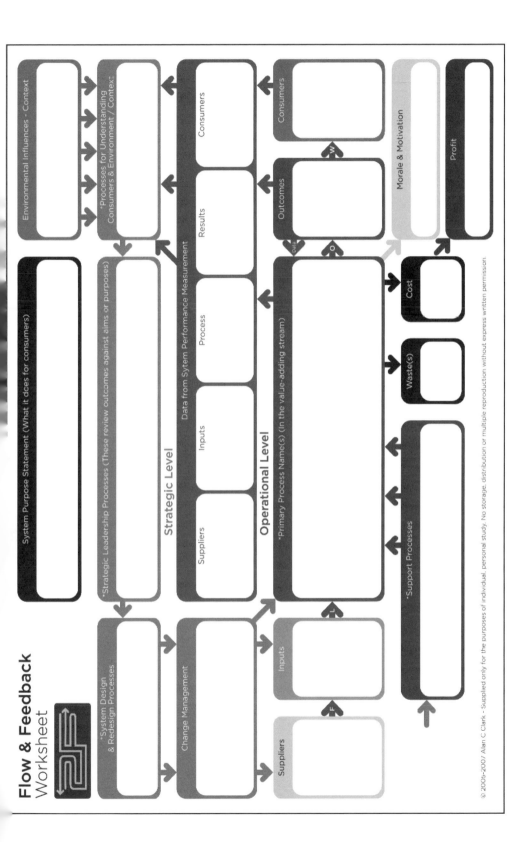

System Purpose Statement (What it does for consumers)

Environmental Influences - Context

Processes for Understanding Consumers & Environment / Context

*Strategic Leadership Processes (These review outcomes against aims or purposes)

Strategic Level

Data from System Performance Measurement

| Suppliers | Inputs | Process | Results | Consumers |

Operational Level

*Primary Process Name(s) (In the value-adding stream)

Consumers

Outcomes

Morale & Motivation

Profit

Cost

Waste(s)

*Support Processes

*System Design & Redesign Processes

Change Management

Inputs

Suppliers

Your notes